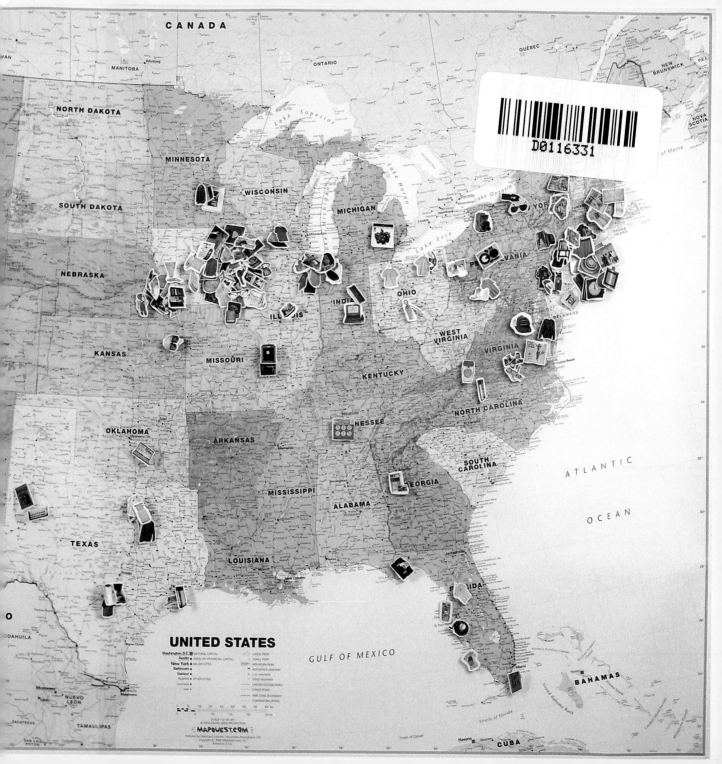

All My Life For Sale
Final Sales: $4,906.52
Auctions Ended: Aug-11-01
Number of Bids: 1,927
Iowa City, Iowa

all my life for sale

John D. Freyer

BLOOMSBURY

Although technically this book is a work of nonfiction, the information contained within comes from memory, and John Freyer's memory has been known to be filled with hyperbole and exaggeration. His friend Kris once observed that if you multiply or divide any number John uses to bolster his argument by a factor of two that new number better represents the truth. For example, if John were to explain to you that it took about ten hours for him to drive from Iowa City to New York City, you could use the above formula to determine that it's in actuality a twenty-hour trip. We apologize in advance for any of his memories that don't quite agree with your own.

Published by Bloomsbury, New York and London
Distributed to the trade by Holtzbrinck Publishers

Cataloging-in-Publication Data is available from
the Library of Congress

ISBN 1-58234-251-2
First U.S. Edition 2002
9 8 7 6 5 4 3 2 1

Typeset in Minion and Syntax
Designed by John D. Freyer
Printed and bound by
C&C Offset Printing Co., Ltd., Hong Kong

Yesterday I started going though Sasha's bookshelves looking at how other "authors" had written their acknowledgment pages. They thanked their agents, partners, children, publishers, and editors. Since the making of this book was only possible with the active involvement of so many different people, my list of thank yous could fill the next five pages and even then I will have left people out. Indeed I do need to thank my agent Bill Clegg for calling me in Iowa and telling me that he thought my project might make an interesting book, my editor Colin Dickerman for helping sort through the hundreds of items and stories I posted on the web, and Bloomsbury for taking the risk of letting me make exactly the book I wanted to make. But there are so many more people that made this project possible. Everyone who bid on an item from my life played a role in the making of this book, especially the bidders who eventually invited me into their homes and shared their stories with me. I need to thank my family for bidding on their own Christmas gifts, a testament to the types of things that they have had to put up with over the years; Margaret Stratton for admitting someone with a degree in government into an art photography program; the University of Iowa Center for the Book, who after some negotiation has accepted the creation of this book as my final project; my friends all over the country who watched me put the things that they gave me up for sale on eBay; Julie and Sara for late night talks about fonts and paste; Kembrew for his soul; Trey and Bekah for having to hear about nearly every art idea I ever had, and then watching those ideas take their sometimes unrecognizable forms; and finally I need to thank Sasha Waters, whose little house with a white picket fence has made me decide to stop starting over.

For Jack

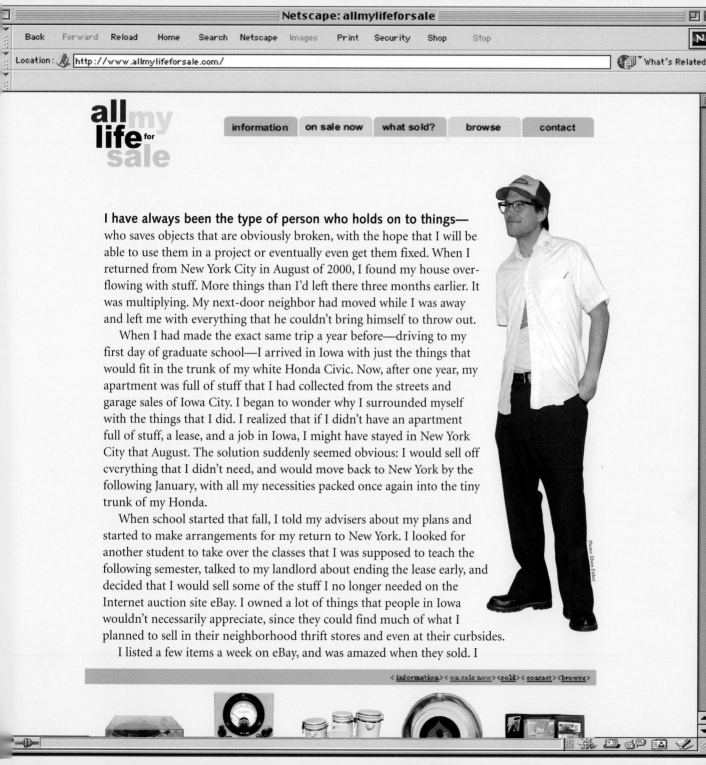

all my life for sale

information   on sale now   what sold?   browse   contact

I have always been the type of person who holds on to things— who saves objects that are obviously broken, with the hope that I will be able to use them in a project or eventually even get them fixed. When I returned from New York City in August of 2000, I found my house overflowing with stuff. More things than I'd left there three months earlier. It was multiplying. My next-door neighbor had moved while I was away and left me with everything that he couldn't bring himself to throw out.

When I had made the exact same trip a year before—driving to my first day of graduate school—I arrived in Iowa with just the things that would fit in the trunk of my white Honda Civic. Now, after one year, my apartment was full of stuff that I had collected from the streets and garage sales of Iowa City. I began to wonder why I surrounded myself with the things that I did. I realized that if I didn't have an apartment full of stuff, a lease, and a job in Iowa, I might have stayed in New York City that August. The solution suddenly seemed obvious: I would sell off everything that I didn't need, and would move back to New York by the following January, with all my necessities packed once again into the tiny trunk of my Honda.

When school started that fall, I told my advisers about my plans and started to make arrangements for my return to New York. I looked for another student to take over the classes that I was supposed to teach the following semester, talked to my landlord about ending the lease early, and decided that I would sell some of the stuff I no longer needed on the Internet auction site eBay. I owned a lot of things that people in Iowa wouldn't necessarily appreciate, since they could find much of what I planned to sell in their neighborhood thrift stores and even at their curbsides.

I listed a few items a week on eBay, and was amazed when they sold. I

Photo: Elton Fisher

< information > < on sale now > <sold> < contact > <browse>

started to photograph the objects and write descriptions, and as I did that I couldn't help but think about where each object came from, and why I even had it in the first place. Many of my friends in New York were working for the booming online catalog industry, and spent their days writing copy for the products in their catalogs. This was the summer of 2000, and everyone I went to college with was making money hand over fist in the dot-com boom doing pretty basic Web design. Every week the news reported on the latest twenty-seven-year-old millionaires, art museums were forming for-profit online businesses, anything and everything was going dot-com.

I decided that I needed my own dot-com, that it would be interesting if I built an online catalog like the one my friends were building for Martha Stewart, but this one would have the lost and found objects that cluttered my Midwestern apartment. In early September, I sat down at my computer and started typing in catchy titles to a domain-registry service. Yardsale.com—not available. Garagesale.com—not available. Junkyard, junksale, housesale, lifesale, lifeforsale, allforsale, everythingsale—all not available. This was the era of people buying up domain names and selling them to corporations for millions of dollars. It seemed like every name was already registered. I eventually entered allmylifeforsale.com and the computer replied AVAILABLE.

Available. I registered it on the spot, thinking that someone else would get it if I didn't snap it up. Who was I kidding? Did I really think that there was someone else out there trying to come up with a domain name to build an online catalog that featured the random objects that occupied his life?

After the name was registered, I wasn't sure what I should do. My original plan was to sell off my unwanted objects and move what I had left to New York, but the domain name that I registered didn't really allow for such maneuvering. It didn't say some-of-my unwanted-stuff-from-the-curb for sale, it emphatically said *all*. Having sold a few things on eBay, I started looking around my house, thinking about how long it would take for me to actually go through and auction every single thing I owned. I was overwhelmed, and my reasons for the sale in the first place were obscured by the daunting logistics of the task.

I knew I would need help if I was going to finish the sale by the end of December, so I invited everyone I knew—and even some total strangers—to my house in October for an inventory party. I handed everyone a clipboard and a handful of tags, and instructed them to tag things that they thought were "representative of my life in Iowa City." The party lasted into the early morning, and in the end more than six hundred items were tagged. This was exactly the structure that I needed. The inventory list included things that were found in boxes under my bed, items from my underwear drawer, things from my bathroom medicine cabinet—objects that I didn't even know I had. I now had a detailed list of possessions that was pretty representative of the "all" that the newly registered domain name specified.

I started to go through all of the items that were tagged—from my favorite shirts to the canned food in my cabinet. As I photographed each item, I reflected on the role that it played in my life and the stories that almost every object made me remember if I spent just a little bit of time with it.

I was immersed in these objects' histories, and started to think about what would happen when I no longer owned them. As an undergraduate political science major, I wrote a thesis about the use of consumer profiling in business and government surveillance. Such profiling presumes that if you could collect information about how people consume goods and services, you could create a pretty good picture of their personality traits, and might even be able to predict the types of choices that they will make in the future.

The dot-com culture thrived on the idea that it could use the Internet to gather such information. All catalog-store business models included layer upon layer of customer-tracking technology. Some dot-coms were setting up businesses that operated at a considerable loss on the consumer-sales side, while selling consumer information to anyone who would buy it to make up the difference.

The histories contained in the objects that I owned could never be uncovered by the consumer profiles that were attached to me. What would happen to my customer profiles when I no longer owned these things? Would I soon have to forward my junk mail to the people who bought my objects on eBay?

In November, I started to sell items on eBay that I had simultaneously posted to the allmylifeforsale site. The first object I sold was my toaster. I sent it to Bill in Illinois. And almost immediately after I sent it, I wondered if Bill even cared about its history. I started to think about the history Bill would attach to my toaster—would it burn his toast, as it did mine? I also realized that the act of selling these objects would start to change my life in subtle ways. After I sold my toaster, I stopped eating toast.

It was also in November that I came to terms with the fact that there was no way I could finish selling everything I owned by the end of the year. I was able to list about ten items during the entire month of November; at that rate it would take me three years to get through all of the tagged items. So the project that grew out of my desire to leave Iowa was now keeping me there. The objects that prevented me from leaving were still doing so, but the other reasons for leaving soon became irrelevant.

The first items I sold ended up all over the country. The simple act of listing an item on eBay had the potential to distribute that item any-where in the world. I wanted to know more about where all the things I was selling were going, so I started to include a request in the invoice that I sent to high bidders asking them to send me an update on the items they purchased. Some people withdrew from my auctions altogether, but as the sale went on, more and more people were interested in providing information. Over time, I started to receive photographs and stories from the various people who participated in the project, and I posted the updates on the allmylifeforsale site with pictures of the corresponding objects. A genealogy of objects emerged as the project continued, and people who visited the site could get a sense of the histories—old and new—that were attached to my former possessions.

As more people participated, a community seemed to form around allmylifeforsale. I was in almost daily contact with many of the high bidders, and was soon more interested in the people who bought things from me than I was in the objects I was selling. At about this time, I received an invitation to visit my salt shaker in Portland, Maine. I had never been to Maine, and thought about all the other places my stuff had gone that I had never seen, either.

So, halfway through the project, I sent out another message to all the high bidders saying that I was going to get in my car with whatever was left after the sale, and would like to visit all the people who had bought things from me. Within a week, I had received forty invitations to visit my former possessions. As the project continued, I started to include the prospect of my visit directly into the eBay listings, so the new owner would know in advance that their purchase might lead to a visit from me.

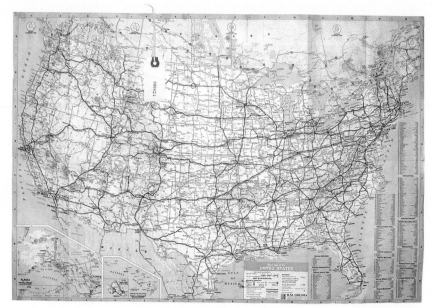

Tag # 000028
Map of USA
Auction Ended: Jan-25-01
Cambridge, Massachusetts
Page: 55

By the end, I had received more than one hundred invitations from all over the world. London, Melbourne, Tokyo, and New York—I didn't know how I would even go about it. On August 1, 2001, my apartment was completely empty; I had sold about six hundred items on eBay, another six hundred or so at a yard sale the week before, and I still had a few boxes of things left. I brought what I could to the local dump and put the remaining items into storage in various friends' basements.

I decided to start my trip in the Midwest and head east from there. The first visits seemed to go pretty well. I really liked the new owners of my things, and was happy to see that my objects were usually more prominently displayed and appreciated than they were when they were in my cluttered apartment. In the first leg of the trip, I tended to stay a few days in each place, trying to meet up with as many people as possible.

As I met more people, the awkwardness of meeting strangers started to wear off. I got comfortable staying in strangers' homes, meeting new people every day. Some might say too comfortable. By the end of the trip, I would help myself to food in the high bidder's refrigerator without a second thought. As I traveled, I posted daily updates on an online travelogue I created at temporama.com.

I was in the Northeast on September 11 in fact, I was in New York City. I had woken up at seven A.M. without an alarm at my friend Maya's house on Canal Street, and had decided to get an early start on my drive to Boston. At eight-forty-five I was sitting in traffic listening to WNYC somewhere just inside the Bronx on I-95. I listened to news radio during the entire four-hour drive to Boston, and by the time I arrived I was whipped up into the same panic that most of the country was in.

My last posting to Temporama was on September 10 from New York City, and I started to receive messages from random readers of Temporama—complete strangers—asking me if I was OK. Although I had been posting regularly to the travelogue, I guess I never really thought that people were reading what I wrote. I suddenly realized that I wasn't alone on this journey, that many people were traveling along with me. I posted an update so that readers would know that I was OK, and then I tried to figure out what to do next.

I paused the trip for a few days, and eventually canceled my southern itinerary, heading back to Iowa to figure out whether I should continue. I contacted all the people who had invited me to visit and asked them if I was still invited under the current circumstances. Within a day or two, nearly everyone who had invited me to visit sent a new invitation.

I began my tour again, but the nature of my visits changed considerably as I continued. In the beginning, I would spend half my time trying to compose the right photograph of my former object. After September 11, I stopped caring so much about the objects that I was visiting and started caring more

about the people who invited me. By the time I made it to Austin, Texas, I had been on the road for nearly three months and had slept on floors, couches, and lawns from coast to coast. The six thousand dollars that I'd made from selling nearly everything I owned had been spent on gas, car repairs, and heart-stopping food. After September 11, I always had a few hundred dollars with me in cash for emergency gas and lodging. While in Austin I started to spend that reserve, and I decided it was time to go home.

Although I hadn't made it to everyone who had invited me to visit, I knew that it was time to stop driving. That it was time to stop looking. I realized that my sale had done far more than just provide me the means and the free-dom to escape and start over. In fact, I no longer wanted to escape. I wanted to return to Iowa City and continue the life I'd started there. All too often in my life I had just picked up and left when things got difficult or overwhelming, and started over somewhere else. Upon returning to Iowa in November, I made a decision to finish my graduate study and to finally finish this project, which had gone on for more than a year. I had spent a year and a half contem-plating the things that surrounded me, even after they were long gone. I no longer wanted to move to New York. I now knew that it was possible to engage the broader culture from somewhere besides a big city. After living out of the trunk of my car, location no longer seemed as relevant. I wanted a place to be grounded. I wanted to stop starting over.

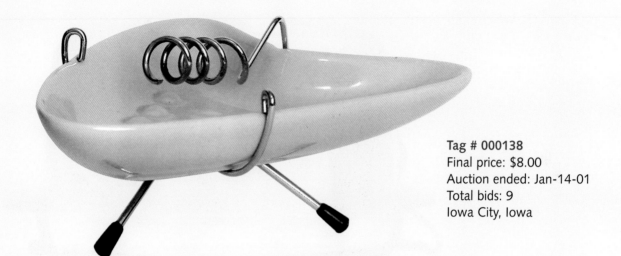

Tag # 000138
Final price: $8.00
Auction ended: Jan-14-01
Total bids: 9
Iowa City, Iowa

Kidney Ashtray: Pink porcelain ashtray on a steel-wire frame. I don't smoke, and I'm not really sure who gave this to me. I almost took up smoking for a while because this ashtray is so damn cool. All right, sometimes I smoke, but I never inhale.

Update: My friend Courtenay owns this ashtray now. She was with me in the car when I started thinking about selling the contents of my apartment on eBay. We were driving back to Iowa from New York City, where I had worked over the summer. Somewhere along the way, Ohio I think, I realized that the contents of the trunk of my car were the same as when I'd arrived in Iowa the year before. I realized on Interstate 80 that if I didn't have an apartment over-flowing with stuff to return to, I most likely wouldn't have left New York City that summer at all, that the objects I owned were making decisions for me. At some point in our conversation Courtenay told me that it was the worst idea that she had ever heard, and that maybe she should drive for a while.

Tag # 000091
Final price: $11.50
Auction ended: Nov-18-00
Total bids: 7
Grayslake, Illinois

Sunbeam Toaster: Polished Stainless Steel Toaster. I have toasted 327 slices of bread in this fine Iowa-bought toasting device. This replaces my first chrome toaster, which I found for free at a garage sale in Iowa City. I sent the first toaster to Bekah, who nearly burned down her house when she plugged it in. This one works much better.

Update: Bill bought this toaster, the first item that I sold. It was his bid that made me think the project might actually work. It made me aware that eBay truly was a huge audience, and that if you put something up for sale, eventually somebody would buy it. This sale also made me realize that as this project continued, my life would start to change in subtle ways. After Bill bought my toaster I stopped eating toast. Does Bill eat more toast?

Tag # 000176
Final price: $1.00
Auction ended: Dec-19-00
Total bids: 1
Washington, D.C.

Harrison Ford's Hat: Krissi gave me this hat in the summer of 1999 in Jackson Hole, Wyoming. She received the hat from her friend who was the caretaker at Mr. Ford's ranch in Jackson Hole. I wore this hat quite a bit. It is foam and mesh, good padding for falling on your head while skateboarding. Did I mention that the hat says SANCHEZ CONTRACTING AND SLAUGHTER-ING? So are they a company certified to build houses and kill livestock?

Update: Ed works for Dick Armey in the House of Representatives. I don't think that he is allowed to wear this hat to work, but he had it on when I met him for dinner last December. He is probably as far to the right as I am to the left, but we get along really well. I met him when he made the mistake of sign-ing up to live in a vegetarian co-op at Hamilton College. I'm not sure what he was thinking, but throughout that year Ed, Trey, and I made weekly pilgrim-ages down to the golden arches in town to get our fix of flesh.

Tag # 000082
Final price: $11.51
Auction ended: Dec-19-00
Total bids: 15
Iowa City, Iowa

Road Trip with John Freyer: "Round-trip road trip (650 miles or more) with John in the Honda." I'm not sure who tagged this item, but it seems fitting. I have driven cross country ten times or so in the last ten years. Every six months I have to drive at least eighteen hours or I start to go crazy. Every time I go to the mall in Iowa City, I have to drive on I-80. I can't help but think that I could just keep driving and in less than a day I could be in New York City or San Francisco. I will pick the high bidder up, and hopefully they will be able to drive and share expenses.

Update: On the day that Sasha won this auction she called me and shouted "Omaha Zoo" into the receiver. In September we finally drove to Omaha and visited the Henry Doorly Zoo. It is actually quite impressive; they have an aquarium with a shark tank where you walk through a fifty-foot glass tube with fairly large sharks swimming above your head. We drove to Omaha on secondary roads and stopped for lunch in Winterset, the seat of Madison County, Iowa, home to the famous *Bridges of Madison County*. The chicken-fried steak was delicious.

Tag # 000015
Final price: $39.00
Auction ended: Dec-24-00
Total bids: 21
Tampa, Florida

Update: Neighbor Ben now lives in Atlanta, Georgia, and every time I see him he has something else to give me. For my birthday this year he gave me his grandfather's Underwood Typewriter. He made me promise that I wouldn't sell it. The high bidder on this phone never sent me an update, but their eBay user name sounded like they ran a vintage technology store, so I'm sure that they resold it to someone somewhere.

Brown Telephone: Telephone from 1970s, donut shaped, touch-tone. When I returned from New York City this summer I found my house filled with boxes of stuff from the basement of Neighbor Ben. Neighbor Ben was the second person that I met in Iowa City, and he lived next door to me during all of last year. On Sundays he would always cook up some sort of red beans and rice or jambalaya, and call my house when it was done. When he moved he left me boxes of things that he thought I would appreciate. One of which was this excellent brown phone.

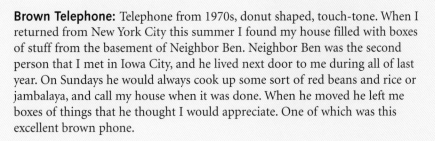

Tag # 000676
Final Price: $1.00
Auction Ended: Dec-19-00
Total bids: 1
Iowa City, Iowa

Prescription Safety Glasses: Real sixties-style safety glasses. Micah bought me these glasses for a dollar one time when we were in Jackson Hole, Wyoming, during a spontaneous road trip that started after last call at George's Bar in Iowa City. I convinced a lens company in the mall to put prescription lenses into them so I could wear them. I had to offer the technician a beer, because they don't normally fill old frames with new lenses. Beer is always a very useful bargaining chip when trying to get a fellow wage-worker to do you a favor.

Green Polyester Pants: Part 2 of a formerly two-piece green suit. These are from the green polyester suit that I vowed to get married in. I wore this hip suit to my Hamilton College graduation, to my brother Mark's wedding, and on the ski slopes of the Snowbird Ski Resort. I mailed this suit to myself in Iowa this spring only to have the UPS folks lose half the contents of the package, most notably the jacket part of this suit. So it's now just a pair of green pants that I was planning on getting married in. Will you get married in these?

Updates: Margaret Stratton bought both the pants and the glasses. She hasn't worn them out on the town yet, but if I ever get married I'm going to ask her to attend in these fine green pants. I recently found a slightly nicer blue gray polyester suit at a local thrift store. It's a three piece so I might actually be able to pass it off as a fine enough suit to marry in. As for the glasses, she refuses to pay me for them, so she doesn't have to take them off my face.

Tag # 000025
Final Price: $6.50
Auction Ended: Dec-19-00
Total number of bids: 6
Iowa City, Iowa

Update: Dave Ellsworth lives in Iowa City. The first items that I sold on allmylifeforsale mostly sold to my friends and family. I'm not sure which is worse, selling things to a stranger and never seeing my stuff again or walking into the Foxhead and seeing my jacket slung over Dave's stool. Sometimes I think about putting the jacket on and walking out the door. He was even wearing Joey's blue jacket when I ran into him in Austin, Texas at the South by Southwest Film festival last month.

Tag # 000006
Final price: $5.00
Auction ended: Nov-25-00
Total bids: 2
Iowa City, Iowa

Blue "Working Gear" Jacket, Size XL: The jacket is soft, broken in, and insulated. It belonged to Bekah's friend Joey, who is a Samoan black belt and has appeared in numerous punk rock music videos. Bekah gave me the jacket last January and I wore it through most of the winter last year. It is very warm when worn with layers.

Update: A drink with Shari was the first "experience" that I sold on eBay. Nearly every day of the ten-day auction she would call me and tell me what her total was up to. In the first five days of the auction the bidding was in pennies: $3.77, $5.22, $6.52. All of the bidder names were familiar too, friends of ours mostly. But on the sixth day, I received a frantic call from Shari. "We have a problem," she stated matter-of-factly, explaining that the bidding had gone up twenty dollars in fifteen minutes and was still rising. "Problem?" I asked, thinking about how many one-dollar PBRs that $26.52 would buy me at the Foxhead. She explained that the bidding war was between some guy named Brian and an eBay user with an X-rated username. Over the next five days Shari tried to convince our friend Kembrew and others to outbid the two eBayers locked in the fierce bidding war over her. She accused various friends of being the X-rated eBay user, one of whom had never heard of my project and had never used eBay in his life. In the end Brian was the high bidder and turned out to be a friend of Shari's, and the mysterious eBayer ended up being Kembrew. Throughout my project Kembrew would roll out his sick little name to bid on various experiences that I listed.

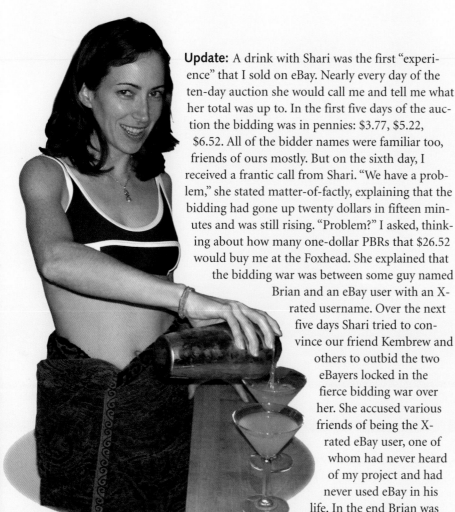

Tag # 000018
Final price: $52.00
Auction ended: Dec-19-00
Total bids: 30
San Francisco, California

Drinks with Shari DeGraw: Cheap date with young working professional at George's Bar or the Foxhead, Iowa City, Iowa. My friend Shari DeGraw teaches fine printing at the University of Iowa Center for the Book. If you like to talk about fonts, paper, or leading, this is a great item to bid on. Keep in mind that in the great state of Iowa one can buy Pabst Blue Ribbon at the Foxhead for one dollar. When I got back from New York City I bought six PBRs just so I could see how much more beer you get for six dollars in Iowa. Six dollars for a bottle of Bud?

Tag # 000678
Final price: $2.62
Auction ended: Dec-19-00
Total bids: 2
Iowa City, Iowa

Wool Socks: Gray heavy winter socks. I borrowed these socks from Anna and Derrick after a cold and snowy trip to Utica to go the Utica Club Brewery, the Uptown Grill, and the Utica Salvation Army. How I convinced two friends to drive an hour to Utica I'm still not sure, but in the end we had free beer, cheeseburgers, and lots of new thrift, and I got a pair of warm socks out of the deal.

Update: I sold somebody else's used socks. There were a few moments during this project that I stopped for minute to think about what it was that I was doing. The day Jason bought my used socks was one such moment. They were just socks, right? I didn't want to give them to him. I didn't want to surrender the memory of where they came from. The simple thought of where they came from occurred to me each and every time I put them on. I haven't talked to Anna or Derrick in a year or two now, and over the last year I haven't thought of them as much.

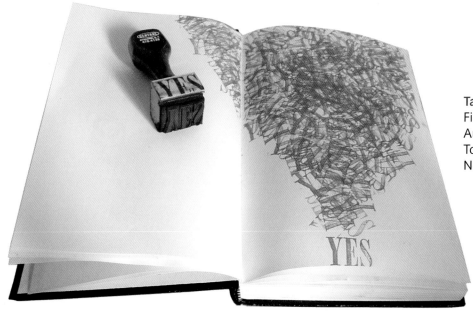

Tag # 000141
Final Price: $6.37
Auction Ended: Dec-28-00
Total bids: 6
New York, New York

YES Stamp: My therapist tells me that I have a problem with saying yes too much. She says that I am so eager to please others that I don't know when to say No. This fall I was working three-quarter time for the University of Iowa, taking a full class load, and trying to do freelance work for Wind-Up Films. It is hard to say no when I have this YES stamp around.

Update: Maya has my YES stamp, and she tells me that she too says YES too much now. She used my stamp to contribute pages to the thousand-journal project, where journals were sent around the world using the Internet to make connections. As for me, I still can't say no, and my therapist has left for another job, so I have no one to tell me to stop saying yes.

Tag # 000878
Final price: $6.74
Auction ended: Dec-24-00
Total bids: 6
Saratoga Springs, New York

Update: Even though she goes to school there, my sister hates Canada. It's a little strange, actually; I find myself defending Canada when I am around her. She is often asked to answer for "her" government's actions in the world. It didn't use to bother her when her friends asked where she kept her gun, but now she gets a little annoyed.

Lauren's Christmas Gift: Lauren is my stepsister. I have known her since she was three, when I fed her so much spaghetti that she called me over to her high chair and proceeded to throw up all over me. That, of course, was a long time ago. She is now a freshman at a university in Canada. Why Canada? I ask that every waking moment. I have an unjustified fear of our neighbors to the north and I am afraid that they will indoctrinate my little sister. Next thing you know she'll be watching *ABC Nightly News* and *Beverly Hills 90210*, not to mention listening to Céline Dion. This fall she got the top grade on a test on Canadian political structure. She knows more about Canadian politics than Canadians. If they let her cross the border she might be able to bid high and get her Christmas gift.

Sarah's Christmas Gift: Sarah is my half sister. I never really got the distinction between half, step, and whole as far as siblings go. She is the daughter of my stepmother and my father, and she's as whole a sister as I can imagine. Are half sisters easier to baby-sit, or change the diaper of? Sarah is now a teenager, which makes me feel really old. Thank God that my brother, Paul, and I have given her mother such good on-the-job training for dealing with teenagers; I'm sure she now knows all the ways that kids can sneak out of the house at night. (Sarah, if you want to make sure you can get back in after sneaking out, leave the side door on the garage unlocked, but make sure you leave a clear path so that they don't hear you fumbling through the garage. If you get caught just tell them you were working on your bicycle. I think that worked for me once. Oh, and Sarah, you better be the highest bidder, because I think you will actually like your gift from me this year.)

Update: This was the top seller of my family's Christmas gifts last year. After Christmas the eBayers, who were in a bidding war with my stepmother, wanted to know what it was they had been bidding on. Sadly, most of the gifts I gave to my family that year were T-shirts I'd made picturing the items that I was selling on allmylifeforsale. Sarah received a shirt with my ice cube tray printed on the front. Ironically, she gave me ice cube trays for Christmas to replace the ones I sold.

Tag # 000904
Final price: $26.07
Auction ended: Dec-24-00
Total bids: 11
Saratoga Springs, New York

Tag # 000905
Final price: $5.50
Auction ended: Dec-24-00
Total bids: 6
Saratoga Springs, New York

Barb's Christmas Gift: Barb is my stepmother, and when I moved in with her and my dad I was twelve years old. How would you like to have to deal with just the angst-filled teen years of your children? She didn't get to see me when I was a cute little baby crawling around the floor. No, she got to deal with a bratty, self-absorbed teenager who spent three or four years pressing her buttons. Add to that my older brother Paul, and how she ever made it through our teen years I will never know. Well, I bought Barb this gift as a way to make that all up to her, and hopefully she will be the highest bidder or she will be reminded of a teenager who she thought had actually grown up!

Update: Barb was designated as my family's proxy bidder. On Christmas Eve she started placing bids on all of the family gifts that I listed. She was surprised to find that all of the gifts had been bid on, and soon discovered how important it is to keep an eye on the eBay auctions that you want to win. In the last five minutes of bidding, someone nearly outbid her on every single item. She quickly outbid the random strangers on the first few gifts, but found herself locked in a war for my sister Sarah's gift, which eventually sold for $26.07 (see previous item).

Update: I don't remember what I gave Mark for Christmas. It kind of looks book-shaped, doesn't it? On Christmas Eve we usually drive to his farmhouse in upstate New York, but in 2000 we were late because Barb was busy bidding on the family's Christmas gifts. I stopped by Mark's house last summer when I passed through on my way to Maine. I had never been to his house in the summer. It was warm, green, and sunny.

Tag # 000910
Final price: $10.50
Auction ended: Dec-24-00
Total bids: 8
Saratoga Springs, New York

Mark's Christmas Gift: Mark was the first of the Freyer "miracles." For some reason their doctor told my folks that they would be unable to have children, so they adopted a boy and a girl and lived their lives as usual. That is, until the "miracle" that was Mark's birth, which that same doctor said was a fluke and couldn't happen again. That is, until Paul came along.… Mmm, two miracles in three years, how likely is that? Well, how about my birth a year and half later? I don't believe in miracles. In fact, I think today they would call it malpractice.

17

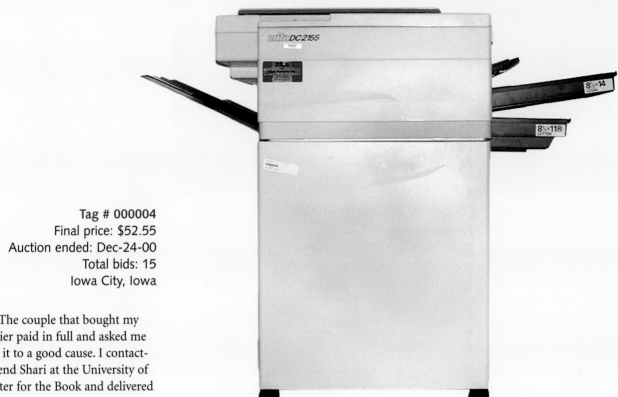

Tag # 000004
Final price: $52.55
Auction ended: Dec-24-00
Total bids: 15
Iowa City, Iowa

Update: The couple that bought my photocopier paid in full and asked me to donate it to a good cause. I contacted my friend Shari at the University of Iowa Center for the Book and delivered it to them last January. My hope is that it will be used to make inexpensive artist books and zines, but I was told it still needs to be serviced and sits unused in the UICB Type Kitchen.

Mita DC-2155 Office Copier: Full-size eleven-by-seventeen Mita Office Copier, three paper cartridges, and full-size rolling copy cart. I bought this used photocopier at the University of Iowa Surplus. Joe originally wanted four hundred dollars for it but I offered significantly less, and then I only had fifty dollars in my bank account. So I wrote him a check for that amount, promised to pay the rest later, and took the copier home. The following week I paid half of what I owed and Joe settled my debt. If you haven't been already, make sure you visit the University of Iowa Surplus sale on Thursdays from ten to six.

Tag # 000220
Final price: $5.75
Auction ended: Jan-05-01
Total bids: 5
Atlanta, Georgia

Driver Zine and Tape: Legacy keys are very useful indeed. When I was at Hamilton College, Thomas (the same guy who gave me my phone list, page 115) gave me keys #377 and #419, which opened the external entrance to the art building and the art office. With such a set of keys one might think that I would try and change my grades or pull pranks on the art faculty, but I was only interested in one thing, the photocopier. Free, unlimited photocopying—that may explain why my sophomore year was filled with the production of five or six "premier" issues of assorted topical zines.

Trey and I produced *Driver* during the final week of our senior year. By this time the photocopier in the art office required a password because the "faculty had abused their photocopying privileges by making more than two-hundred-thousand copies during the '93/'94 school year." Some thought it was the art historians; others thought it was the studio faculty. Trey and I distributed this limited run to most of our friends and said good-bye. We also took turns putting songs onto a mix tape. Trey collected indie rock and I collected disco, so this tape could be the worst combination of music since MTV actually played music videos.

Update: When I moved to Iowa, Lincoln gave me a legacy key to the art building. I still look both ways before I use it so as to not get caught and have the locks changed on me. Neighbor Ben won the auction, but when I went to mail the item to him I couldn't find the tape that was supposed to be in the case. I am still trying to track someone down who has a copy of it so I can send it to him. It still sits in an addressed envelope waiting for a tape to fill the case. Sorry, Ben.

Tag # 000211
Final price: $15.50
Auction ended: Dec-25-00
Total bids: 7
Belmont, California

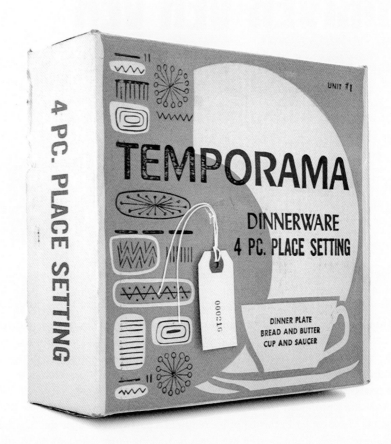

Temporama Dinnerware, Four-Piece Setting: When I lived in Syracuse I would go to the flea market every Saturday. One week I saw a woman walking around with a number of Temporama boxes. I must have offered her five or six times what she had just paid for them from another vendor, because she quickly took my money and handed them over. I think I fell for the packaging, and I soon found myself using the name for the online travelogue that I started in the spring of 1997. I never opened all of the boxes and sent the remaining unopened settings to Trey, Bekah, and Saori.

Update: Dan is a collector of Temporama dishware and my last box added to the reserve collection he keeps in storage, just in case. He's collected enough dishes to host a fairly large dinner party. He is going to send me photographs of his first Temporama dinner party. I think the next time I go on the road I am going to invite myself to dinner at the house of anyone with Temporama dishware.

Update: Jenn and her daughter Paine were the first to send me an update on an item that I sold. They sent me a photograph of my salt shaker on the shelf above their stove and told me that they were regularly using my HyVee salt. At the end of the update they invited me to visit. I suddenly realized that a community might be forming around the objects that I was shipping around the country. I decided to take them up on their offer and soon started to inform the high bidders on my other objects that I might want to visit them too. I stopped by Jenn and Paine's house on September 3, 2001.

Tag # 000203
Final price: $1.00
Auction ended: Dec-24-00
Total bids: 1
Portland, Maine

Salt Shaker and Salt: Iodized salt, glass-and-steel shaker. The salt? I bought it at the HyVee grocery store in Iowa City, Iowa. The shaker? I think it's from my grandparents' estate. After my grandmother passed away in 1996, I moved to Syracuse, New York, with Lanethea. My Aunt Patsy and Uncle Chuck had rented a storage space for much of the stuff from my grandparents' apartment in Florida. Having just moved into a new apartment, I took much of the kitchen stuff, including this salt shaker.

Tag # 000068
Final price: $4.75
Auction ended: Dec-24-00
Total bids: 4
New York, New York

Brown Zipper Shirt: This is 100 percent pure polyester. It's brown, it's polyester, it's got a zipper with a ring handle. I have worn this shirt in many a disco club. I can guarantee that if you wear this shirt you will be able to stay on beat when you dance. Mark Sottilaro has one thing to say about pure polyester: "hot in the summer, cold in the winter." If comfort were so important then we would all be wearing pajamas. This brown shirt is hot.

Update: The selling off of my polyester clothing may have been the best outcome of this project. I no longer have to worry about sending a static charge through the hands of the people I meet. And people no longer confuse me with an extra in an episode of *The Rockford Files*. I have found, however, that it is hard to stay on beat in 100 percent cotton.

Tag # 000005
Final price: $15.77
Auction ended: Dec-24-00
Total bids: 15
Region: Bellingham, Washington

D&D Auto Body Nylon Winter Jacket: Green nylon jacket with D&D AUTO BODY, UTICA NY in golden embroidery. Front snap closures and zip-down hood, yellow fuzz insulation, looks great. I purchased this jacket in Utica at the world's best Salvation Army. I once wore this jacket in an ice storm in Saratoga Springs, New York. The nylon was so slippery that I was able to slide down the entire length of Caroline Street on my stomach.

Update: Ralph bought my only winter jacket in January of 2001. In one of the last e-mails that I received from him, he said that every time he watched the Weather Channel he felt a little guilty about buying my winter coat. That winter was one of the coldest on record in Iowa, with wind-chill factors averaging about twenty below zero for most of the month of January. Ralph was enrolled in auto-body-repair school last winter. I wonder if my jacket helped him pass his exams.

Chunky Soup: Cooking is therapy for me. I like to spend my Sundays reading Molly O'Neill and cooking some big stewlike meal for myself and Neighbor Ben. During the last few months I have been overwhelmed with work and have spent my Sundays trying to catch up. That means that I have had to eat prepared foods more than I would like to. I learned to cook at the Keehn Cooperative at Hamilton College (above left). It was there that I learned a very important cooking lesson. DO NOT MULTIPLY SPICES! Trey and I usually signed up for cooking duties and one night we were responsible for making "Chicken with Forty Garlics." The recipe called for forty cloves of garlic for a four-person recipe. We were cooking for forty people, so I did some simple multiplication and peeled four-hundred cloves of garlic. Our new specialty, "Chicken with Four Hundred Garlics," didn't really go over that well. Trey and I had to open all the windows in the kitchen and we spent the following week eating all of the leftover chicken. I didn't get sick all semester long that year.

Update: I submitted this can to the annual book-arts show at Arts Iowa City last spring. It was on display with the handmade artist books and fine-press editions. I made the mistake of leaving the can down there for a week after the exhibition closed and I think someone may have prepared themselves a nice hot lunch. Margaret, who was the high bidder, has been asking me about the can for the last month or so. I think Campbell's has redesigned its packaging, so I can't just go to the store and buy a new can of soup.

Tag # 000234
Final price: $2.25
Auction ended: Dec-28-00
Total bids: 3
Iowa City, Iowa

Tag # 000052
Final price: $26.01
Auction ended: Dec-28-00
Total bids: 18
Dallas, Texas

Science-Related Bottles: Lots of little science bottles. *Surplus* is a word that you will read often in my descriptions. Iowa Surplus is overflowing with stuff: beautiful, used stuff, from oak flat files to used science equipment. I have a little bit of a problem: I never miss a Thursday Surplus sale and I never leave empty-handed. Even now, as I'm selling everything that I own, I'm still buying stuff at Surplus. These are my favorite little science bottles.

Update: Last week I went to Surplus and found a set of the very same bottles on the same table where I bought these a year before. After a while I have started to realize that the things at Surplus seem to replenish themselves every single week. Julie was a regular bidder on items from my life; I think these were the first items she bought from me. Last December my sister Sarah found herself bidding against Julie for her own Christmas gift.

Tag # 000089
Final price: $1.00
Auction ended: Dec-24-00
Total bids: 1
Boston, Massachusetts

Match Books: Do you collect matchbooks, or do you just smoke? I don't really do either. I like to collect free stuff from places I go, because it reminds me of where I've been. It is also great to have someone tell you that they have been there too. My favorite restaurant in New York City is the Great Jones Café on Great Jones Street. They cook a nearly perfect cheeseburger and sweet potato fries. Here are a few matchbooks that I grabbed on the road. Bid high and you'll know if you have been where I have been.

Update: I was supposed to stay with Rob when I went to Boston last fall, but since I arrived on September 11, there was no way that I could stop and talk to him about my former matchbook collection. I ended up driving back to my family's house in upstate New York after making the six-hour drive from New York City to Boston that same morning. It was a terrible drive.

Tag # 000102
Final price: $3.01
Auction ended: Dec-25-00
Total bids: 4
New York, New York

Ice Cube Trays: There is no real detailed history to this particular part of my life for sale, but I can tell you that this piece of equipment needs to be used in conjunction with a refrigerator. I will include the instructions for making ice and will also include all of the ice currently in the tray. I have used ice from this tray to cool burns from my cast-iron skillet, to help chill Maker's Mark for long heart-to-heart chats with my friend Sara Langworthy, and even for cooling down a room-temperature beer or two.

Update: I put the trays in doubled-up Ziploc bags and put Maya's address on them. When I mailed them the ice was still solid, but Maya tells me that it arrived in a more liquid state three days later. She still has the trays on her desk in her office and tells me that during the summer the Ziploc bags turned into a mini-terrarium, with the water vapor clinging to the sides and raining down into the trays. I must have forgotten to give her the directions for making ice.

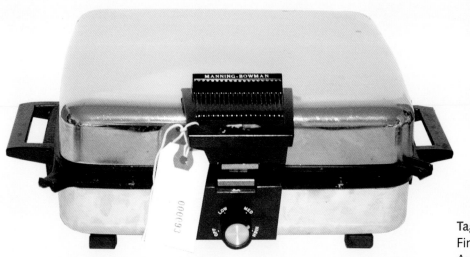

Tag # 000093
Final price: $4.75
Auction ended: Jan-05-01
Total bids: 9
Enterprise, Florida

Waffle Iron and Grill: Waffles? I've never made them. I would love to tell you a story about the breakfast I made for someone who stayed at my house, but this never happened. In fact, I have only one breakfast story worth telling, and it involves my cast-iron skillet, Neighbor Ben, and my friend Courtenay. As soon as you close the door to my apartment it locks automatically. During the first week that I lived there I locked myself out seven times—that's once a day. Thank God it was summer and Landlord Dan was doing construction on the house. Well, the trend continued, the ladders were gone, the windows were locked, and my landlord started to charge me every time I locked myself out. So I gave a copy of my key to Neighbor Ben. And from that point on he kind of made himself at home. Often I would come home to find a few less PBRs in my fridge or Ben doing homework on my computer. One morning after I had spent the night at my girlfriend's house, I found Courtenay and Ben in my kitchen making a full-on Sunday breakfast. The high bidder on this item should be forewarned that Ben might show up at their door wanting waffles.

Update: Rani is a dietician of sorts and used my waffle iron to test out her new low-carbohydrate recipe for waffles. She was unwilling to send me the "soon-to-be-published" recipe, but I imagine there is a particular market that would be interested in a low-carb waffle recipe. I think that I might give Neighbor Ben Rani's address.

Tag # 000099
Final price: $4.00
Auction ended: Dec-25-00
Total bids: 6
Brooklyn, New York

CHiPs Sunglasses: In July of 1999 I was staying in Government Camp in Mount Hood, Oregon. It snowed on July 4 that year. I was working with Wind-Up Films and lost both pairs of sunglasses that we got from our sponsors. So I had to go down to the supermarket and buy these. They kind of work, but I don't think they do much to filter out UV rays. I mostly wear them to the post office with my hooded sweatshirt.

Update: Jen recently graduated from Syracuse University and now works in an art gallery and at Paper Tiger television in New York City. I used to work with her at Light Work's Community Darkrooms. I taught her how to mop. She has made art videos about shopping malls and Levittown, New York, and occasionally she sends me copies of her most recent projects.

Wyoming T-shirt: In January of 2000 I had just returned from visiting my family for Christmas when I had a drink at a bar with Micah, whom I had had a crush on since the day I met her. During the conversation we discovered that we had mutual friends in Jackson Hole, Wyoming, and started to wonder if we could just drive out there. We went back and forth about how broke we were and our work schedules and such. At last call at George's Bar, we decided that she would pay for gas if I drove my car. So we went home to gather up enough stuff for two days and hit the road at about three A.M. or so. We arrived in Jackson eighteen hours later and stayed at Krissi's house. While in Jackson I discovered that Micah had a crush on me too. Which led me to believe in love at first sight and caused me to lose all sense of reason for the next three months. I found this shirt at the same thrift store where I bought my first western shirt in the summer of 1999. I didn't have even the dollar it cost, so I let Micah buy it. She looked pretty good in it too. I fell in love with her, almost bought two tickets to Las Vegas to marry her, and three months later we broke each other's hearts. I found this shirt under my bed this summer after I returned from New York.

Tag # 000285
Final price: $10.50
Auction ended: Dec-28-00
Total bids: 13
Iowa City, Iowa

Update: James Galvin is one of the writers in the Iowa Writers' Workshop. He is originally from Wyoming, and much of his writing is about his experiences growing up there. A friend of his bought this shirt for him as a gift. Although it is a little tight on him, he sometimes wears it around town. The last time I saw him in town he was a little puzzled by my request for an update on "my" Wyoming shirt. The shirt is now back in Wyoming at his ranch— appropriately, in range of the AM radio station that the shirt advertises.

Roasted Cuttlefish: When Saori Hoshi returned to Japan after going to school at Hamilton College, she complained that she was a victim of a "fish attack"—i.e., Saori's mother assumed that she would have to make up for Saori's three years without fish by feeding her all fish, all the time. One day I opened a package from Saori to find my own "fish attack." I'm not sure what a roasted cuttlefish is, but it looks a little gross and I'm not sure where the expiration date is. It has looked really nice hanging on my wall for the last few years.

Tag # 000078
Final price: $4.25
Auction ended: Dec-24-00
Total bids: 2
Tampa, Florida

Update: The cuttlefish moved from Tampa to Tennessee last fall, and the new owner's cat couldn't resist its own form of "fish attack." It tore the salted snack to pieces from its exhibition space on the family refrigerator. When I was anywhere near the ocean last fall I too fell victim to a self-imposed "attack." Having lived in Iowa for two years and only having access to frozen fish, I ordered fish for nearly every meal as I drove down the West Coast. It was so nice to finally get back into the middle of the country and order a simple dish like meat loaf.

Update: Margaret Stratton is one of the reasons I came to graduate school in Iowa in the first place. She was the high bidder on many of the things I listed in the beginning of the project, including my favorite green pants, my glasses, my can of Chunky Soup, and these cocktail parasols. I don't think that she ever paid me for any of the things she won, and I have yet to deliver even one of her new objects. I see her nearly every day and never fail to mention that she owes me about twelve dollars for the items. She says she never has the money on her, but I know she is just telling me that so she doesn't have to be the one to take my glasses off my face. I think I'll give her these parasols today, no charge.

Tag # 000165
Final price: $7.02
Auction ended: Dec-24-00
Total bids: 8
Iowa City, Iowa

Cocktail Parasols: These were in a box under my bed with lots of little things that I have collected over the years. I have never used them, but I have a few cocktail shakers. The person who tagged these was a little taken aback by the idea of rummaging through a box of personal stuff under someone's bed. I guess it was a little weird for me to watch all these people go through my stuff too. But he rummaged and this is what he thought would be representative of me. Bekah gave me these.

John Freyer's Birthday Party: My birthday is on December 31, and every year I am reminded by my father that I was the best gift he received in 1972. He was able to claim me as a dependent for all of 1972 even though I was only alive for two hours. Normally, I spend New Year's somewhere in New York City, with Trey and Bekah, but this year I am spending it in Iowa City at the Motley Cow Café. Since I will not be in New York City on my birthday, my friend Maya is throwing me a birthday party at Recess in downtown New York on Thursday, December 28, at eight-thirty. This item is an opportunity to be "John Freyer" at my birthday party, which I will attend as well. The highest bidder will receive all the free drinks that people might buy me as well as any gifts and cards. Recess is on Spring Street between Greenwich and Renwick (the old Bell Café); you can get there by taking the C/E to Spring Street, and then walking west.

Update: I wasn't sure what would happen when I met the high bidder from this auction. It closed three hours before the party, and I was afraid that I wouldn't be able to contact the high bidder until after the party was over. Brian returned my e-mail almost instantaneously, and I invited him to dinner at Maya's house. When he showed up he said he was relieved that he could hear a crowd of people in Maya's apartment. While he was on the subway to Maya's he imagined approaching a silent, poorly lit door. I introduced him to my friends at dinner and showed him a stack of photographs of all of my friends who would be at the party at the bar around the corner. He memorized their names and faces and greeted my friends by name when they walked in the door. At some point in the evening I brought out a birthday cake and we all sang "Happy Birthday" to "John". A few weeks later I received a message from one of my friends saying that they were hanging out with "John Freyer 2". Brian is now friends with a good number of my friends in New York. I think they might have thrown him a birthday party at Recess this year.

Tag # 000727
Final price: $1.25
Auction ended: Dec-28-00
Total bids: 2
New York, New York

Brown "Cliff" Coat: Brown work coat with yellow CLIFF embroidery. I have had this jacket for more than eight years, and every time I have moved it has gone with me. I wear it all year round; it has light insulation and is amazingly warm in the winter and cool in the summer. I used to write a weekly column called *Cliff Notes* for *The Spectator* at Hamilton College. I wrote opposite Derrick Johns, a conservative Republican. Every week we would write about similar issues from differing perspectives. I would call for the end of the fraternity system and he would write about the proud fraternal traditions. He would write about not wanting to see gay people kissing and I about not wanting to see straight people holding hands. My father once received a note from one of his fraternity brothers wondering if his son John was really advocating the elimination of fraternities at Hamilton. I was, and Hamilton did reform their fraternity system, and this is the coat I wrote those columns in.

Update: Greg works for an interactive-media company in Minnesota and just informed me that the last time that he went to Madison, Wisconsin, "Cliff" was stolen from the restaurant he was eating in. I wonder if the new owner knows the history of that object? He or she stole it before Greg even attached his own history to it. I told Greg that I would keep an eye out for our jacket the next time I am in Madison. "Cliff" thieves beware!

Tag # 000175
Final price: $29.50
Auction ended: Jan-02-01
Total bids: 5
Arden Hills, Minnesota

Tag # 000193
Final price: $15.50
Auction ended: Jan-02-01
Total bids: 8
Albany, California

Answering Machine Tape: I'm not sure who was the last person to call my answering machine, but I know there are a few really long messages from my ex-girlfriend Micah and my mother, that probably haven't been overwritten. I'd rather not listen to them again myself, but if you are the voyeur type this is the item for you.

Update: Morgan is a musician and producer and thought that she might be able to use samples from my answering machine in the music that she creates. In her last message to me she reminded me of the five messages in a row that my mother left on my machine debating the pros and cons of Ralph Nader. Morgan said she would send me a copy of anything she makes using my tape.

Tag # 000289
Final price: $4.55
Auction ended: Jan-05-01
Total bids: 4
Sterling, Virginia

Las Vegas Souvenir Glass: Black-and-gold-painted glass with Las Vegas icons from top to bottom. I almost bought two tickets to Las Vegas last February, in order to get married to my girlfriend Micah. I received this glass as a gift from her three days after we officially broke up in late March.

Update: Elle wrote to tell me that the Vegas glass arrived broken into five or six pieces. She too nearly made the mistake of getting married in Las Vegas at about the same time as me. It now sits in the box that I sent it in, somewhere under her bed. Which is where the glass was in my house when someone tagged it in October—under my bed in a box.

Tag # 000238
Final price: $2.50
Auction ended: Jan-05-01
Total bids: 3
Homewood, Illinois

Update: Greg asked me if I could talk to my dad about sending him the five cans of leftover Spanish peanuts. My ham now sits in his kitchen pantry ready to serve four. I'm not sure what the expiration date on canned meats usually is. I can't imagine longer than two or three years. After consulting with my dad I told Greg that the peanuts were gone and that if he planned on eating the ham to do it quickly. I almost ate the remaining ham at my father's house when I stayed there for a few days.

Millennium Canned Ham: Last year at this time I was seriously convinced that the world could end on New Year's Day. So instead of going to the big bash in Times Square, I joined my friends Bekah, Zarela, and Doug, and a few of their friends, out on Long Island to prepare what I thought might be my last supper. Well, I was wrong, really wrong, and I got my folks so worked up about it that my dad went out and bought a few weeks' worth of provisions. But rather than buy a ready-made disaster kit, he came up with his own emergency list, including five cans of Spanish peanuts, a few one-liter bottles of tonic water, and three canned hams. This fall I opened a care package from my family to find this fine Danish ham courtesy of the Y2K rations that I had advised my dad to buy. I chose not to eat it just in case the real millennium comes this year.

Tag # 000166
Final price: $2.25
Auction ended: Jan-14-01
Total bids: 2
Dallas, Texas

White Toy Cadillac: Bekah sent me this car eight years ago, and I have carried it with me on many of my road trips. I may not drive a big car, but I have this one in my pocket when I'm driving. This is a great item for any size kid.

Update: Julie sent me a doctored photograph where she inserted my white Cadillac into a still image from the Zapruder film. She wanted my car to have a place in local Texas history. The image was a little disturbing, to say the least, but it was one of the first updates that I received, so I was happy to have it. I think she might do a series of doctored historical photographs where my Cadillac makes an appearance.

Tag # 000034
Final price: $1.50
Auction ended: Jan-14-01
Total bids: 2
Lubbock, Texas

Update: Cris is a graduate student in theater in Lubbock, Texas. When I visited last fall we stopped by a conference hosted by the Society of Photographic Education, where we met up with Jim Stone, an artist who I know through my work at Light Work. Cris has never seen the Bread and Puppet Theater perform, but teaches his undergraduate students about their role in alternative community-based theater. There is still no word on whether or not the Bread and Puppet festival will resurface.

Bread and Puppet Posters: My brother took me to see the Bread and Puppet Domestic Resurrection Circus one summer in Glover, Vermont. Every summer the Bread and Puppet theater used to host an annual festival, and even though they only announced the festival via word of mouth, each consecutive year that I went the crowds got larger and larger and larger. The last Bread and Puppet festival took place in the summer of 1998. It was the last because many of the attendees were young Phish heads who thought that the Bread and Puppet festival was another Dead show, and in 1998 one person died in a fist fight, and some idiot lit a van on fire. So they canceled the festival for good. But they still run small programs all summer long so make sure you make a trip to the North East Kingdom of Vermont.

Tag # 000013
Final price: $3.25
Auction ended: Jan-14-01
Total bids: 3
San Francisco, California

Refrigerator Magnets: Assorted refrigerator magnets, including *Power Puff Girls, Star Wars, Star Trek,* and homemade family. I have way too many magnets. One year for Christmas I scanned my family slides from the 1970s and made magnets out of the images, pictures of my three brothers and my sister Marnie.

Update: This year Sasha and I did the Christmas tour of the Northeast. We stopped at my sister Marnie's house, my dad's house in Saratoga, Sasha's mom's house on the Upper West Side, and then her dad's place in lower Manhattan. Her sister Nell, who bought them, complained about how ineffective the magnets were. Apparently, the Power Puff Girls' magnetic pull is so weak that she can't hold anything up with them.

Tag # 000178
Final price: $61.00
Auction ended: Jan-27-01
Total bids: 13
Iowa City, Iowa

Kitchen Table: When I moved to Iowa, I lived at Margaret Stratton's house until I was able to find an apartment. Every lease in this town turns over on August 1. Margaret's friend Anne and I spent the days before and after the first driving around in Margaret's truck picking up all kinds of abandoned furniture and the like. One morning she called me from work and said that she had seen a fifties chrome table at the end of Dodge Street. I brought a screwdriver and made the table fit in my little Honda. It needed some work but nothing that a little Ajax couldn't clean up. I could tell other stories about this table, but I think I should just stop with this.

Update: I am writing this exactly one year from the day that this auction closed. Sasha was the highest bidder and our friends continue to laugh at us when we explain that I made her write me a check for the whole amount. Sasha and I had recently started dating at the time and no one thought that I would make her pay me for the table. But I did, I had to, because other bidders would have paid for the table in full and would have paid the shipping to boot. A year later the table now sits in the little house that I share with Sasha on Church Street in Iowa City. I moved in after I returned from visiting the participants of this project and spend much of my time in her house writing at the very table I sold her a year ago today.

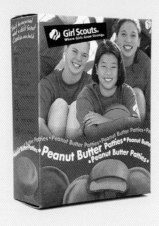

Tag # 000729
Final price: $2.00
Auction ended: Jan-14-01
Total bids: 3
Mumbles, Swansea, United Kingdom

Update: Mike is a crew member on a lifeboat team in the small village of Mumbles (population 130—slightly more than the town that my niece Avery is from). He bought the "biscuits", as he called them, for his son Huw, who often helps around the lifeboat station. They received the air-mail package in good time and shared them with the rest of the crew of the station. I sent Avery Mike's address so that she can send him this year's Girl Scout cookie catalog. When I saw Avery this summer there was no sign of "Fat Baby".

Peanut Butter Patties: My niece Avery is in the Brownies, and about a month ago she sent me these Girl Scout cookies as a care package. Avery is the oldest of three beautiful girls that my sister Marnie and her husband, Michael, are raising in an old farmhouse in upstate New York. The girls call me "Scary Uncle Johnny", which is a little disconcerting, because I consider myself to be pretty good with kids. Avery carries around "Fat Baby", which is an old set of infant-footed pajamas filled with all of her stuffed animals. It is this weird, bulging, awkwardly shaped figure with mini-teddy bears for hands and a different bear for a head each time "Fat Baby" is reassembled.

Update: Scott used to tend bar with me at the Motley Cow Café, and started to wear my tan guayabera while on duty. Tom, the owner, never sent him home for not wearing a suit. I don't think that the Senate has changed its dress code to the guayabera yet, but I think the idea may be included in one of the pending campaign-finance-reform bills.

Tag # 000271
Final price: $10.50
Auction ended: Jan-25-01
Total bids: 6
Iowa City, Iowa

Tan Guayabera: When I was an intern in the Senate Judiciary Committee in Washington, I tried to convince the staffers there that in Cuba the guayabera that I wore to work one day would be considered a business suit. (Suits are the required dress code for interns in the United States Senate.) They didn't buy my argument and sent me home.

Tag # 000880
Final price: $20.50
Auction ended: Jan-25-01
Total bids: 14
New York, New York

Update: After I sold this on eBay I sent the auctions listing to my thesis adviser and to the president of Hamilton College. They both sent rather puzzled responses to my sale. I'm not sure they understood what I was up to, but neither did I at the time. The new owner, Skye, promised to read it. He must have, because I haven't heard from him since. Maybe he wrote the president of my college too, asking how they could have let me graduate.

My Hamilton College Thesis:

Information Technologies and Their Role in Surveillance Societies. This paper is a little out of date terminology-wise, but many of the predictions that I made in 1994 have been pretty right on. Back then I still called the Internet "the information superhighway", and most of my interactions with the Net came through the Gopher system and then Mosaic. The paper talks about how information technology is used to gather personal information in an effort to control people. I reviewed literature by Foucault and also looked at Jeremy Bentham's *Panopticon*. My current project, allmylifeforsale, is informed by my research into information technologies. Part of this project is to see what happens when all of the information collected about my spending patterns and the like is radically changed. If I no longer own the things that supposedly define the type of consumer that I am, will I still consume the same goods and services? Or should the telemarketers start to call the people who have bought my life? It's not a bad read if you can deal with the "information superhighway" language. I still have to thank Trey and Lanethea for proofreading this document.

Hamilton College

Information Technologies
and
Their Role in Surveillance Societies

A thesis submitted in partia
of the requirement
the degree of Bachel

Depart

Tag #000127
Final price: $12.51
Auction ended: Jan-25-01
Total bids: 12
New York, New York

Make Your Booty Itch Tape: Dave Broda is one of the founding members of Light Work and the Community Darkrooms. He works for the photography services department at Syracuse University and he has the best record collection I have ever seen— every James Brown record ever pressed and house music to drool over. We used to trade tapes back and forth and this is one of the ones that he gave me. It's a damn good tape with lots of old funk. He DJs at parties at the Creamery and Sculpture Space in Utica, New York.

Update: Many of the people who bought items from me bought more than one thing. Skye was on track to buy five or six from the bidding list that I reviewed in late January last year. He ended up with my Hamilton College thesis and this fine tape. Both are pretty representative of my interests. The post office returned the package to me twice because they said his address didn't exist. His only update to me came when the package finally arrived with both items. He said that he planned on listening to the tape while reading the thesis. I'm not sure I ever intended the two to be combined in such a way, but maybe my thesis adviser would have changed my grade had he accompanied his reading with disco.

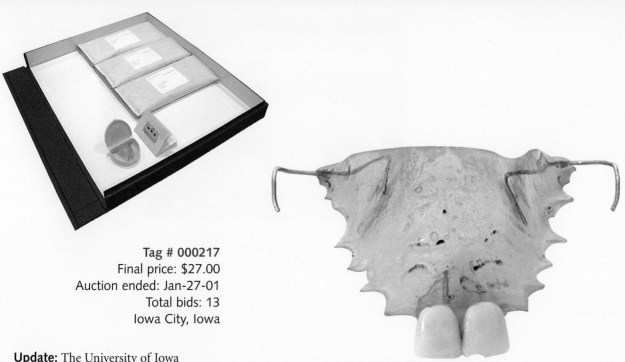

Tag # 000217
Final price: $27.00
Auction ended: Jan-27-01
Total bids: 13
Iowa City, Iowa

Update: The University of Iowa Museum of Art purchased my two front teeth. It was the first museum to take interest in allmylifeforsale and this fall featured my travelogue project, Temporama, as its first online exhibition. A few weeks after they received the teeth in the mail they sent me this photograph of the company they now keep in the archival box where they are stored.

False Teeth: Two slightly used false front teeth. When I was seven I had the nicest set of pearly white front teeth. That was until 1980, when on Easter Sunday my family went to Bellevue Country Club for brunch. After eating a pound or two of peel-and-eat shrimp and some roast beef, I joined my three brothers and sister Marnie outside to run around the golf course in our Easter Sunday best. I didn't get very far. As I crossed from the first tee to the ninth green, I tripped over a wire strung between the trees and fell face-forward onto the golf-cart path. So of course I ran in to cry to my mother, not knowing that I had knocked my teeth out. For the next hour all of the Easter Sunday diners were crawling around the golf course looking for John Freyer's two front teeth. Needless to say, we did not find them that day. After a week of sifting though my poop, in case I'd swallowed them, we gave up and I was fitted for false teeth. I now have teeth permanently implanted and I don't think I'll need these anymore. I will throw in a brown plastic case for the highest bidder.

Tag #000888
Final price: $18.50
Auction ended: Jan-25-01
Total bids: 8
St. Paul, Minnesota

Photograph of Heather Hibbard: This is a photograph that I took of my friend Heather in an abandoned diner on the side of Route 22 in upstate New York. It is hand-printed on fiber-based paper and is mounted and matted on museum board. This is one of my favorite photographs because of the way the light falls on the old tile floor. Heather is now in graduate school pursuing a master's in education so she can teach in upstate New York. I don't think that this diner is still there. I'm not sure where it went, but when I was in California working on my ski film, I ate at a diner in Truckee, California, that had been shipped in four years previously from somewhere upstate; I always wondered if it was the same one.

Update: Kim has my photograph in the "black-and-white photography" section of her house. My friend Heather is hung directly across from a photograph of the Ramones, fine company indeed. When I visited St. Paul this summer, I called Kim and told her that I was going to be in town. She gave me directions to her house and I almost dropped the phone when she told me the cross street: Davern. That's my middle name, and I had never met anyone who knew very much about its history. I always thought it was a family name. I think some of my family moved to Minnesota in the late 1800s.

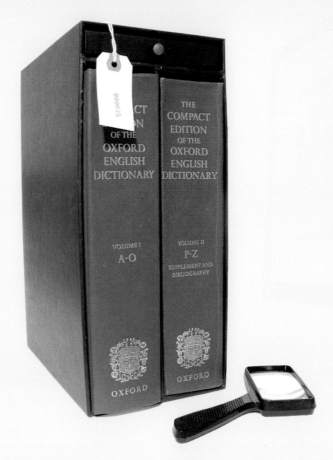

Tag # 000035
Final price: $183.52
Auction ended: Jan-27-01
Total bids: 16
Iowa City, Iowa

OED: I bought this at Margaret Stratton's yard sale one fall, and I have used it once. I heard something on NPR about the word with the most definitions in the English language, so I dusted off the *OED* and looked up "set", of which there are three or four pages of definitions. Three or four pages of definitions so small that you need a magnifying glass to read them. You may notice while reading through this project that I am in bad need of a dictionary. Well, that may be true, but the *OED* is too much book for me. Where are all the English majors?

Update: During Margaret's garage sale, people would come up and offer two dollars for "the dictionary," at which we would laugh. But shopper after shopper would offer similar amounts, which made Margaret and me wonder if she had set the price too high. Well, in the end, I paid her fifty dollars for it, and as I discovered on the open market of eBay, its value was far higher than the garage-sale shoppers determined that late-fall afternoon. It ended up being the most expensive single item that I sold. Jessica, a fellow student in the photography program, won the *OED*, has since started taking nonfiction writing classes, and may soon major in English instead of photography. I think my *OED* made the difference. She recently told me that she was using the *OED* as a weight for books she was making.

Tag # 000556
Final price: $15.01
Auction ended: Feb-05-01
Total bids: 15
Brooklyn, New York

Update: My friend Amanda now owns this great old tape. I haven't talked to her in a little while. She is in a midwifery program at Columbia and right in the middle of her second year. I didn't meet Amanda until I lived in New York in the summer of 2000, but she quickly became one of my closest friends. Within a few months she knew just about every one of my friends who owned a copy of this tape. She still runs into Bekah downtown sometimes; I wonder if she told her that she has the original master for the tape that Bekah and I made more than ten years ago.

Pin-O-Rama **Tape:** This is the tape that changed my life. Bekah and I made this tape with her small record collection at Hamilton College. We included many soul classics on side A, including "Let's Get It On", "Further on Down the Road", "Outstanding", and "Ohh Child", and on the B side we had the hip-hop of the day, including "Who's Gonna Take the Weight?" and "Juice". Almost all of my friends at Hamilton had a copy of this tape, and this is the original master. It was this tape that led me to start collecting records and got me hooked on disco and soul, which led to dance, jazz, and the like. Bekah and I used to trade tapes every few months when we were buying lots of records. Even when I'm making tapes for other people, I can't help but decide what to play based on whether or not Bekah already knows that song. All of my tapes are filled with music that I didn't think Bekah had at the time. This is the best tape I ever made.

Stainless Steel Thermos: This is the greatest thermos in the world. It has accompanied me in my car for more than one thousand miles and keeps me caffeinated for the eighteen-hour drives to New York City that I often feel like making. Lanethea gave me this for Christmas one year. She always got me the nicest gifts. Me, I'm always for the best deal, but she knew how to shop for quality. One night when I was in Utah I was invited to spend the night in the patrol shack at the top of the Snowbird Ski Resort. We made a big dinner for everyone and when we woke up I realized that I had a thermos full of coffee that I had packed the previous morning. Well, it was still warm twenty-four hours later, even at fourteen thousand feet. I guess I have a lot of cold coffee to look forward to.

Update: In June a producer from PBS was doing a story on the variety of items that sell on eBay and asked me if I could put her in contact with anyone from the New York area who had bought something from my project. I contacted a number of the folks in the New York City area, including the new owner of this thermos. My e-mail to him was returned to me as undeliverable, so I did a Google search for his name to see if I could find a forwarding address. It turns out that the former president of the Jewish Defense League owns my thermos. I haven't heard anything from him since I sent the thermos, but I'm sure it keeps his coffee warm.

Tag # 000293
Final price: $42.72
Auction ended: Feb-02-01
Total bids: 25
Bronx, New York

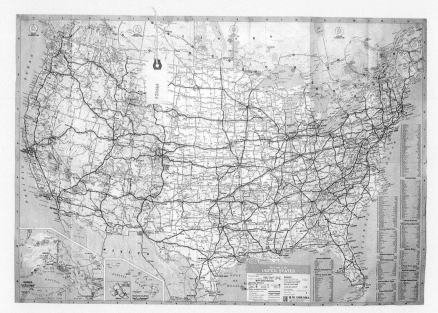

Tag # 000028
Final price: $25.01
Auction ended: Jan-25-01
Total bids: 13
Cambridge, Massachusetts

Map of USA: I've highlighted all the routes that I have driven. When I was nineteen, I somehow convinced my friends Kristin and Molly that Trey and I should accompany them on their road trip to Colorado. I called my folks and told them not to expect me home for a while, and jumped in the car with a day pack full of stuff and headed west on I-90, which turns into I-80, and then south to I-70. We saw Colorado and Taos, New Mexico, and from that day on I was hooked. In the years since, I have driven in nearly every state. Trey and I borrowed this map from Bekah and I have been highlighting the roads I have been on ever since—more than three-hundred-thousand miles.

Update: Nirosha uses my map as inspiration to travel. She originally intended to take a cross-country road trip, but the last dispatch that I received from her said that she and the map were on their way to Phnom Penh, Cambodia. I still remember the pink highlighted highways on that map and have been thinking recently about contacting her and asking her to highlight the new roads I have been on since she acquired it.

Tag # 000048
Final price: $15.50
Auction ended: Jan-29-01
Total bids: 5
Chicago Heights, Illinois

Cast-Iron Skillet: This was the first piece of cookware that I purchased when I moved here. I bought it new and have strictly followed the directions for its care. A properly seasoned cast-iron skillet will last a lifetime, adds needed iron to every meal, and is truly a nonstick cooking surface. I think there was a Teflon conspiracy to get America's housewives to throw out their mothers' cast-iron skillets. Somehow my mother was convinced to get rid of her mother's cast iron and replace it with pots and pans that could barely last five years. Maybe it was our obsession with cleanliness that also led to the demise of cast iron. Cleaning a properly seasoned pan requires hot water and a soft brush, and the use of dish soap is actually discouraged because it removes the layers of seasoning that make the pan nonstick.

Update: The new owner of this pan promised not to use soap in her new skillet, otherwise I wouldn't have sent it to her. For my birthday this year Sasha bought me a new skillet, and the directions for maintaining it have changed since the last time I seasoned a skillet. Now, according to Lodge, the leading manufacturer of cast iron in the world, it is OK to use a small amount of dish soap when you clean the pan. If you ask me, it's probably not a good idea, but I imagine it is hard to convince people that not using antibacterial detergent is proper maintenance.

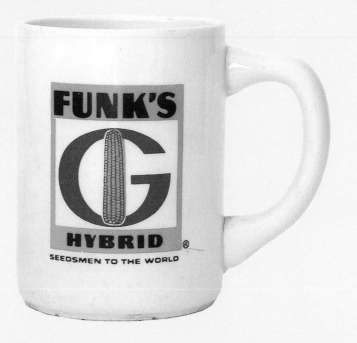

Tag # 000040
Final price: $20.50
Auction ended: Jan-28-01
Total bids: 20
New York, New York

G-Funk's Hybrid Mug: When I first found out that there was a company called Funk's Hybrid, I was on a mission to collect anything and everything with that logo on it. As a collector of funk and disco records, G-Funk's Corn seemed pretty damn cool. This summer when I returned from New York, Micah gave me this mug. It's pretty nice. I'm not sure if Funk's still sells seeds or not, but I'm always on the lookout for new jackets, hats, and mugs.

Update: This mug has a new home on the sixth floor of the Chrysler Building, one of my favorite buildings in New York. This was one of the most requested items to be put up for auction. One bidder wrote me about his embarrassing attempt to smuggle a similar mug out of his father-in-law's house. His wife likes to remind him of the incident often. Apparently not all G-Funk mug owners are as willing to part with them as I was.

Tag # 000329
Final price: $2.25
Auction ended: Jan-27-01
Total bids: 3
New York, New York

U.S. Army Chair: The University of Iowa had a U.S. Army office at one point, and UI Surplus is filled with steel case desks and the like that used to fill that office. This wooden chair is one of the first chairs that I had in my apartment in Iowa City. I learned early on that the way to get a good deal from Joe at UI Surplus is to promise to give something a "good home". Who will have a good home for this chair? It needs a little love here and there, but nothing a little wood glue won't fix. It's my favorite chair in the kitchen. I read the paper in the morning in this chair.

Update: When Roxanne found out that it would cost more than forty dollars to ship this $2.50 chair from Iowa to New Jersey, she told me I should donate the chair to a "good cause". I drove around town for two weeks with the box tied to the roof of my car. I decided to send the oversize boxed chair unsolicited to the Franklin Furnace Artist Book Collection at the Museum of Modern Art. When Franklin Furnace donated its collection of artist books to MoMA in 1993, it did so with the requirement that MoMA continue to maintain an open accessions policy, taking any item that an artist submits as a book. I submitted my chair.

"It's a Strike" Bowling Belt Buckle: I have a number of belts and buckles and this is one of my favorites. I love bowling. I have about five or six bowling shirts. When I was in high school they offered bowling as part of the gym classes. Bowling was so popular that they decided to pair it with aerobics, the least popular class. I was the first guy to take the bowling class in five years because no guys were willing to go through the aerobics section first. Well, my high-school sweetheart was certainly embarrassed when she had to watch her boyfriend lead the aerobics class. I kind of got into it. I felt like "Mr. Body", telling the girls to "make it burn". "Now the other leg." "One and two—and the other arm."

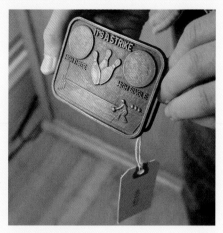

Tag # 000321
Final price: $48.00
Auction ended: Jan-29-01
Total bids: 23
Berkeley, California

Update: Erin and I were both born on December 31. She bought the belt buckle for her boyfriend Danny and when I went to visit them last fall we decided to go bowling. Her father was in the air force, so as a kid Erin spent much of her free time in the bowling alleys that seem to be on air force bases worldwide. I wonder if my Iranian bowling shirt (page 108) came from an air force-base team?

Tag # 000760
Final price: $20.50
Auction ended: Feb-05-01
Total bids: 7
Iowa City, Iowa

Update: Eureka Joe's has since closed. It was across the street from the offices of the publishing company that is now printing this book. My final project for the Center for the Book is the design and layout of the book that you are reading. Trey continues to write poetry and I might try to do another project with him when I am finished with this one. This copy of *Pilgrims 10* sold to one of my former students at the University of Iowa.

Pilgrims 10 **Book:** I am enrolled in the certificate program at the University of Iowa Center for the Book. My first letterpress-printing project was a book of poetry called *Pilgrims 10*, by Trey Sager. It featured ten poems, each titled "Pilgrim". I don't read very much poetry and I think it has challenged my friendship with Trey. This book seemed to be a good way to get involved in his work without having to offer specific feedback on the poems that he was writing. I printed an edition of ninety-nine and we nearly sold out of them at Trey's book-release reading at Eureka Joe's, in the Flatiron district of New York.

Tag # 000209
Final price: £100
Auction ended: Feb-3-01
Total bids: 1
London, United Kingdom

RCA Salt and Pepper Shaker: I received these for Christmas from Bekah. We tend to send each other record-related paraphernalia, and what could be more record-related than RCA salt and pepper shakers. I have never filled these with salt or pepper, but they have always been displayed prominently in my house. I will miss these.

Update: In February a British tabloid discovered my project, downloaded pictures of every single item on my site, and then printed them across two full pages of their evening edition, with a short piece of text mostly lifted from the title page of allmylifeforsale. The next day I received six calls from the BBC and one from a woman named Julia, who only left her name and overseas number. For some reason I returned Julia's call first. She answered the phone and asked me how much I wanted for the "Dog and His Master." When I told her that everything was on sale through eBay, she explained that she had no access to the Internet, but saw the picture in the paper. So I decided to have a one-person auction over the phone. I told her that she could have the salt shakers for whatever price she offered, and when she said one hundred pounds, I tried to talk her down.

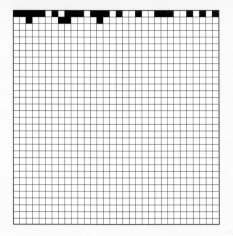

***Every Icon* Digital Art Applet:** On Friday, John Simon came to Iowa City and visited the Digital Worlds Garden at the University of Iowa. He talked about his *Every Icon* project (www.numeral.com), which was featured at the Whitney Biennial in 2000. He sold me a copy of the project, a Java Applet which cycles through every possible combination of images on a thirty-two-by-thirty-two-pixel grid (the standard image size of all computer icons, e.g., the Mac trash can, the folder icon, etc.). The catch is that displaying every icon possible will take the program billions and billions of years. My copy will start calculating *Every Icon* today. The sooner you buy it the sooner you will get to see the final results … if you have a few billion years to wait.

Tag # 000677
Final price: $36.00
Auction ended: Feb-07-01
Total bids: 15
Brooklyn, New York

Update: When I listed this item I included a link directly to the page where John Simon sells personalized copies of his every icon project for $19.95. The new owner paid nearly twice that for my copy. I sent 10 percent of the sale to John Simon and according to the software agreement I can still maintain my own copy of the piece at home.

Stevie Wonder, *Songs in the Key of Life*: Do you not own this record? Well, don't buy it here, go to your local thrift store and buy yourself a copy. This has to be the second most donated album to the Salvation Army stores of the world, and I can't understand why. The first most plentiful album in America's thrift stores is *Whipped Cream and Other Delights,* by Herb Alpert and the Tijuana Brass. Now that was my favorite album when I was eleven or twelve years old. This album is the best album in the world. I'd list all the songs, but if you don't know what's on this record you don't deserve to own it. And since I think you should support your local thrift store instead of eBay, you might as well leave your computer right now and walk down the block, pay your twenty-five cents and listen to it today…. Or you can bid on my copy, wait ten days for the auction to end, go get a money order to pay for the item plus shipping and handling, and then wait two or three additional days for the U.S. Postal Service to deliver it to you….

Tag # 000805
Final price: $2.25
Auction ended: Feb-14-01
Total bids: 2
Brooklyn, New York

Update: Paul and his wife, Renée, decided not to take my advice and bought my copy of *Songs in the Key of Life.* They also bought my copy of John Simon's *Every Icon* project. So when they invited me to visit this fall I brought John along with me for lunch. At lunch I seemed to talk nonstop about everything but the items that they purchased. I told them about the people I had visited thus far while we listened to this album. They are artists, and unlike many of the participants in my project, who were looking for something specifically utilitarian, Paul and Renée wanted items that were symbolic of my project—either that or the thrift stores in their neighborhood were overpriced.

Tag #000106
Final price: $41.00
Auction ended: Feb-01-01
Total bids: 21
Portland, Oregon

Rodchenko Coasters: Bekah gave me these coasters for my birthday. They are from the Museum of Modern Art's Rodchenko exhibition last fall. Bekah works at the Museum of Television and Radio, which is one block away from MoMA, and as a fellow museum worker she gets into all the museums in New York for free. Not a bad friend to have when you like to go to museums.

Update: I was unusually good at arriving in towns when many of the people who bought things from me were going to be away. I believed them for the most part but was recently reminded of the family joke that I actually believed my mother had taken the family's cats and dogs to a farm on Route 20 so that they would have "more space to run around". At my brother Mark's wedding, my siblings informed me that there was no farm, that those cats and dogs went for the big sleep at the vet's office. Lorenzo and his girlfriend told me they were out of town the week in October that I drove through Portland. I believed them.

GAF Super 8 Sound Camera and Three Rolls of Super 8 Sound Film: Just before I left Light Work in February of 1998, someone donated a bunch of rolls of Super 8 Sound film. Since I was going on another road trip with Trey through the South, I bought a few rolls and started my search for a Super 8 Sound Camera. I was kicking myself because I have had two or three sound cameras in the past, but since the film was no longer available I got rid of them. I couldn't find a camera for the film anywhere and I broke down on the day before my trip and went to K&M camera on Twenty-third Street, where I charged $189.00 on my new Household MasterCard. (I had just quit my job, planned on making a ski movie, and had about six hundred dollars in the bank.) Well, Trey and I drove through the South and I shot a few rolls of film. While shooting I noticed a weird noise, so when I was settled in Salt Lake City, I sent it back to K&M. After looking at it they sent it back and said it was fine; I shot another roll and the noise came back. So the next time I was in New York I brought the camera, and it still made the noise as I shot a roll of film one block from the store. When I went into the store, however, it wouldn't make the noise. And the guy thought that I was crazy after already having sent it back to me once. So maybe I am crazy and this camera is as good as the day that I bought it. It is really clean and according the experts at K&M is in prime working condition. I will include the letter from K&M telling me how well it works. I will also include three rolls of Super 8 Sound Film, two K40s and one 160T.

Tag #000762
Final price: $66.00
Auction ended: Feb-01-01
Total bids: 14
Norcross, Georgia

Update: Steven bought my Super 8 camera so that he could continue work on a short film that he started a year or so ago. When I was out visiting people last fall I received a message from him saying that he had talked it over with his production partner and that if I made it as far as Georgia, they would write in a part for me to play. Sadly, I never made it that far, but I'll bet they will still be working on the film the next time I drive through Georgia.

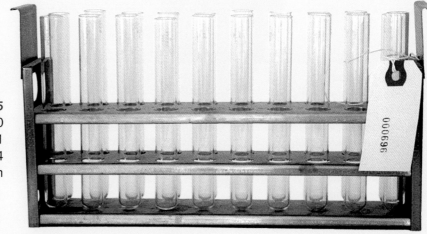

Tag # 000055
Final price: $20.50
Auction ended: Feb-01-01
Total bids: 14
Seattle, Washington

Test Tube Rack with Test Tubes: Are you a mad scientist? Well, I wasn't either until I bought these test tubes at Surplus. Now I am regularly mixing things in test tubes and seeing what transpires. Test tubes are perfect for single servings of salad dressings. Also, I've done some alcohol studies with these, and vodka tastes best out of six-ounce tubes. It's hard to taste scotch though. This stainless steel rack looks cool even without anything in it.

Update: Over the course of my project I learned to how to package breakable items for shipping. I wrapped this item so well that the new owner asked me if I suffered from obsessive-compulsive disorder. Sadly, other things I shipped didn't fair so well. My kitchen canisters, for example (page 144), were so poorly packed that all four arrived in tiny pieces, mixed with the contents of the canisters: flour, sugar, coffee, and cornmeal.

Tag # 000275
Final price: $17.50
Auction ended: Feb-07-01
Total bids: 12
Kalamazoo, Michigan

***Star Wars* Sheet:** This is a full/queen-size flat sheet from the first *Star Wars* movie. Usually I draw the line on buying sheets and undergarments at thrift stores, because you never really know what has happened in someone's pants or under their sheets, but I just had to get this. I have used it as a filter. Filters are things in your house that you test new acquaintances with to find out whether or not you are compatible. An example of a filter date is taking a girl out for a George's cheeseburger. Call me shallow, but if a girl doesn't like to drink cheap beer and eat cheeseburgers then why go much further than the first date? As for this sheet, I put it over my comforter on my bed. It serves as a two-way filter: Either they like it and I think that I could go on another date with them or they hate it and can't believe that a twenty-eight-year-old guy has *Star Wars* sheets. Either way this sheet has served its purpose.

Update: Greg is my age, and when he went away to college his mother donated many of his old childhood things to charity, including his set of *Star Wars* sheets. Ten years later he still reminded them of their mistake and his parents ended up being the high bidders on my used sheet. They sent it to him in Kalamazoo, and I've yet to hear back from him on whether it still has the same filtering properties.

Dear John,

Thanks for the yucky mouth pictures. They sit above my living room windows. Best,
Jason

Tag # 000021
Final price: $41.00
Auction ended: Feb-08-01
Total bids: 16
Portland, Oregon

Update: This summer I visited Jason Livingston in Portland, Oregon. He, too, had reduced what he owned down to what would fit into his Honda Civic, and my dental photographs were part of his core group of possessions. Earlier this year he drew a picture on a napkin of how they were installed in his old apartment. Although they were still in a box when I arrived, he promised to install them in a similar manner in his new house.

Dental Photographs: Four Polaroid transfers from dental-education slides. I used to work at the Community Darkrooms. Each year the Darkrooms have a tag sale to help support their programs, and one year the widow of a professor at the dental school donated all of his slide carousels to the sale. They were full of dental-education slides. I half expected my photograph to be among the pile, since I had often been photographed by my dentists because of my missing two front teeth (page 50). I never found an image of myself, but I made these images from the slides that I liked most.

Tag # 000570
Final price: $3.00
Auction ended: Feb-14-01
Total bids: 3
Denver, Colorado

***Thumb* Zine, Issue 9:** Eric Mast lives in Portland and has published *Thumb* since he was in college at Skidmore. After I graduated from Hamilton, I moved back home and spent six months skateboarding with Eric's housemates Matt and Benj. My first issue of Temporama included excerpts from an issue of *Thumb* that I had contributed to. When Kris and I were in Mount Hood, Oregon, filming *Clay Pigeons,* we often went down to Ozone Records in Portland. Eric helped us find good music to put on the soundtrack, and his friends from the Volume All Stars allowed us to use their music in our film. Eric's mom writes a new music column for *Thumb*; she often says things like "It kind of sounds like they are using broken instruments".

Update: I stopped in Portland on my way to San Francisco. I met up with Eric for dinner and he gave me a copy of his latest edition of *Thumb*. I meant to ask him whether or not Lynn, the high bidder, ever ended up subscribing to *Thumb*. I think she told me that she collected zines before she even bought Eric's zine from me. I'm happy to report that in the latest issue Eric's mom still contributes the music reviews. In her review of the band Chicks on Speed she states, "This is truly awful music too, but in a different sort of way." She's been known to equate bands with the "sounds of a dying cow" or the Beatles, depending on how much she likes the music.

Tag # 000247
Final price: $4.25
Auction ended: Feb-05-01
Total bids: 7
Iowa City, Iowa

Update: As I discovered after I put this up for auction, day traders spend much of their time surfing the Web. I must have received ten or fifteen messages from online traders who didn't appreciate my dig at their "profession". The last time I saw Virginia, I told her that I would make her a print of the shirt that she gave me. It's kind of strange, really, that even though I no longer own these things I still have digital files of them. People still associate the things I used to own with me even though they are all over the country. I finally dropped this shirt off at Margaret's this afternoon.

Virginia's Red Shirt: Virginia is well known in Iowa City. She used to run a consignment shop in town and still has a houseful of stuff from when it was open. I used to work with her at the Motley Cow Café. She gave me this shirt last spring when I spent a few hours on her porch one afternoon drinking PBR cans and enjoying what's left of her great view. Every year or two the hospital next door tears down a few more of the houses in the neighborhood to accommodate parking for the doctors' Lexi and Volvos. This shirt is damn near threadbare, well worn indeed, and in Iowa that usually means hard, honest labor, not like a well-worn shirt from a day trader who buys and sells junk bonds and calls it a job.

Tag # 000284
Final price: $23.00
Auction ended: Feb-12-01
Total bids: 24
Syracuse, New York

Update: Rob Sayre was the first person that I ever hired in my life. He worked with me at Light Work's Community Darkrooms when I was the lab manager there. He was a computer science major and I have been in off-and-on contact with him ever since. The last time I spoke to him he was working on a computer program that would translate a computer image file into an audio file. We talked about releasing a seven-inch record with one of my photographs encoded on the B side, so that the listener would have to record the file to their computer and translate it with his software. I think the recording will contain my photograph of the K-Tel shirt that he now owns.

K-Tel T-shirt: My friend Kembrew has a new nickname based on the posting of this shirt. The name "K-Tel" fits him well, since he is a music critic and has the largest music collection I have ever seen. If you don't know what K-Tel is, then you should not bid on this shirt. My record collection would not be complete without the various hit collections that K-Tel records produced throughout the seventies. Also I think that this is the only item Kembrew wants, so there might be a little bit of a bidding war. Hopefully he won't meet the likes of the eBayer who got into a bidding war with my stepmother for my family's Christmas gifts.

Tag # 000042
Final price: $16.50
Auction ended: Feb-11-01
Total bids: 8
Johnstown, Pennsylvania

Update: After I finished selling the items of my life this summer I made a commitment to myself that I would only replace the things that I needed to travel with. I also decided that I would try to live as secondhand as possible, buying only used clothing and objects. So far I have done pretty well, but I'm afraid that being in one place again reminds me of my tendency to accumulate. Yesterday, I bought a broken laser printer for five dollars. Not everyone who bought things from me wanted to keep me updated on them. My letters to the new owner of this pink shirt no longer get responses.

Pendleton Shirt: Pink 100 percent wool short-sleeve shirt. My friend Sara Langworthy loves this shirt, in part, I think, because her family used to run a mom-and-pop clothing store in Libertyville, IL. They, like many independently operated businesses, recently closed due to the invasion of the Wal-Marts of the world. But when they were open they carried high-quality, American-manufactured dry goods like this fine wool shirt. It's great in the spring and fall, but I wouldn't recommend wool for the humid Iowa summers.

Tag # 000045
Final price: $10.35
Auction ended: Feb-08-01
Total bids: 4
Iowa City, Iowa

George's Cheeseburger with Sara Langworthy: George's Buffet has the best cheeseburger in all of Iowa. A George's cheeseburger with "everything on it" comes simply wrapped in white waxed paper, filled with chopped onion, mustard, ketchup, and garlic salt, all for $2.75. Add a $1.25 Old Style draft, and this is the best-priced date in all of America. Sara Langworthy and I often meet each other for a burger and a beer at George's. The only other bar worth going to in Iowa City is the Foxhead, and Sara hates that bar because every time she goes there she has to reintroduce herself to the same twelve people. How they could forget her I'm not sure. I personally prefer George's too, but the Foxhead does have the one-dollar PBR, which can't be beat when you're living on a graduate school budget. Here is a chance to enjoy two of the best reasons to live in Iowa City, Sara Langworthy and the George's cheeseburger.

Update: About three days after I started this auction I received an automatic message from the eBay gods, explaining that Sara Langworthy is not in fact an object, and that I was not allowed to auction off dates with her on eBay. I made three or four attempts to explain what I was up to, but subsequent "experience" auctions met the same fate. She did meet the high bidder for a cheeseburger last March. Old-Style drafts at George's are now $2.25, and the Foxhead sadly raised their dollar PBRs by a quarter.

  73

Tag # 000199
Final price: $11.00
Auction ended: Feb-11-01
Total bids: 20
Mitcham Junction, Surrey, UK

Update: Pat has my pack of Mexican gum framed and nailed to the wall of his house in Mitcham Junction, England. I haven't heard whether or not he has hosted a pantry potluck yet. When I was on the road I seemed to play the "backseat of my car" potluck game quite a bit. I never liked to arrive empty handed, so I would often take the food that the last person I visited had sent me on my way with and present it to the next person I stayed with.

Gum: I have a drawer in my house where I keep weird food items, and this is where whoever tagged this item must have looked. I received this gum last year when I hosted my Pork Pantry Potluck Party. A pantry potluck is an event where the invited can only bring items that were currently in their cupboards at the time that they received the invitation. I came up with the idea one year when I was hungry and broke and invited friends over for a potluck. Since I couldn't really offer much as far as food, I told them to only bring leftovers from their cupboards. We ended up have a really good meal with old eggnog and whiskey to boot.

Fish Shirt: Fish. Tropical fish, lots of them. I love this shirt. One of my ex-girl-friend's favorite things to do was shop, and by the time we broke up, I was getting into the shopping thing too. Actually I've always been a shopper, but as you can see I mostly shopped secondhand stores. I started shopping retail when I was dating her, and even started to like going to the mall. In fact, after we broke up I went there on my own and even bought stuff from a department store. Forever a changed man. Well, the pendulum has swung back and I'm not a fan of the mall anymore, but this shirt was the turning point in my brief love for firsthand retail shopping. Although discounted, this shirt still cost eight to nine times what I was used to paying for a shirt, but it was worth it because it is covered in tropical fish.

Tag # 000068
Final price: $51.50
Auction ended: Feb-07-01
Total bids: 26
New York, New York

Update: Adam currently works at the *New York Times.* I met him in my first round of visits to New York City last summer. He met me in the main lobby of the Time-Life Building wearing my perfectly fitting tropical-fish shirt. He had just written a cover story about online privacy for *Time,* and here he was meeting a total stranger whom he bought a shirt from on eBay. He has just finished a book about eBay called *The Perfect Store,* which includes a section on my project. Could my shirt be considered a legitimate business expense on his taxes?

Metal Horses: My dad is an owner in a horse stable, sort of. He has about a 2 percent share of a stable that raises thoroughbred racehorses. It's kind of funny, because when one of the stable's horses runs in Saratoga he sits in the "owners'" boxes. Little do the other owners know that he probably owns less than a horseshoe on any of the horses, but he does have a picture of himself in the Winner's Circle with one of "his" winning steeds. Me, I've never really been into horse racing, even after growing up in Saratoga. Once in a while I will place a two-dollar bet on a long shot, but I have never won the big payoff. I'll bet somebody out there wants this little metal figurine.

Tag # 000299
Final price: $23.49
Auction ended: Feb-11-01
Total bids: 16
San Leandro, California

Update: When I drove through Saratoga Springs this summer my father and I went to the track for the last four races of the day. I decided that I should place the twenty-three dollars that I received for the little horses on the longest shots of the day. I placed "win, place, and show" bets on the worst horses in each field and ended up losing every single race. None of the horses from my father's stable ran that day.

Tag # 000058
Final price: $12.57
Auction ended: Feb-14-01
Total bids: 16
Hereford, Texas

Microscope Slide Case: I make books, and when I bought this I thought that I might make a little "book" of images on microscope slides, specifically for viewing with a microscope. I envisioned family portraits made really tiny and then magnified. I am hoping that the high bidder would like to make a collaborative book with me. I will help them troubleshoot how to get the images small, and they will come up with a conceptual reason to put images on microscope slides. That's the thing that I have the most trouble with. I always come up with ideas for projects that I can't really find a way to back up conceptually.

Update: I guess I was asking too much to expect someone to pay for the opportunity to collaborate with me. Although I did not expect 100 percent participation from the high bidders on my items, I kind of expected the new owner of this to invite me to Hereford to make a new project with them. I ended up making a collaborative book called *First Five Free*, with Emily on my way to visit high bidders in Texas.

Tag # 000145
Final price: $3.00
Auction ended: Feb-14-01
Total bids: 7
London, United Kingdom

Update: Steve was the first person from overseas to win an allmylifeforsale auction. Having no idea how much it would cost to ship a brick to London, I told him to send me ten dollars to ship the three-dollar brick. In the end it cost me thirty-five dollars to send it airmail, which seemed the only choice because by sea it would take eight weeks. A month later he sent me a photograph of the brick in his hand above the rooftops of London. When I was in Austin, Texas, this fall I walked by a house with a cardboard sign that read FREE BRICKS. I took one.

Brick: When I first moved here, Thomas Comerford lived in the downstairs apartment; he was the one who introduced me to my landlord, Dan. Dan is a pretty good landlord; he seldom comes around and always gives me enough notice if he needs to get into the apartment. One morning before I lived here Thomas woke up at about seven A.M. or so to the sound of a chain saw. He went outside to discover that Dan had decided to do some early morning yard maintenance. The only problem is that Dan was using a chain saw to cut down the seven-foot sunflowers that Thomas had nurtured since spring. This brick was in my empty apartment when I moved in. I'm not sure if it is considered part of the apartment or not. I hope that Dan doesn't deduct money from my security deposit to replace it.

Tag # 000241
Final price: $6.50
Auction ended: Feb-11-01
Total bids: 6
Denver, Colorado

Wind-Up Films T-shirt: This is a cheap, thin shirt with the Wind-Up Films logo on it. I made it in March of 1999 when Kris and I were on our way to Las Vegas to pitch our film *Clay Pigeons* at the annual ski industry trade show. We made about ten shirts using inkjet iron-on sheets and shirts that we bought at Thrift-town. We left the Thrift-town price tags on them and handed them out to potential sponsors of our film. It kind of worked, most people got a good laugh out of it, and some people eventually kicked down some money so we could finish the film.

Update: After he received it, Eric notified me that the shirt was "as described". I'm not sure what he meant, but it may have been that it was a cheap, thin shirt as promised. This year I designed the Wind-Up Films logo for the sweatshirts that they had professionally produced. Things have certainly changed since the first film that we made four years ago. I arrived in Salt Lake the day of the premier of Wind-Up's third film, *The Flying Circus*. They handed me one of their new sweatshirts that I designed, and I haven't taken it off since. It's cold in Iowa, and I sold my winter coat last December.

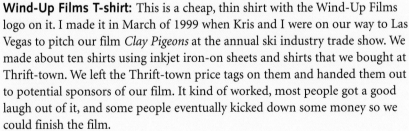

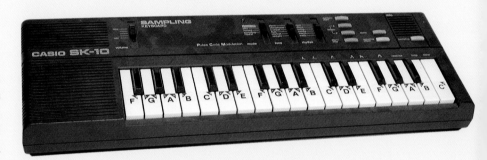

Tag # 000129
Final price: $45.00
Auction ended: Feb-14-01
Total bids: 15
Clarksville, Virginia

Casio SK-10 Sampling Keyboard: When I was a student at Hamilton College I took three video classes from Ella Gant. She gave the best class assignment ever. (Video art instructors take note!) No matter how hard she tried to get us to do interesting work, we would always find a way to turn her video assignments into some sort of music video. It must be frustrating to watch really bad music videos year after year. So one of the first assignments in Video 2 was to make a music video. The catch was that each student had to compose the music themselves, perform the song, and, since the bulk of popular music takes the form of love songs, each song had to be a love song. The other requirement was that the music had to be composed on a cheap Casio keyboard. I created a song to Laurie Pensive, a character that Trey and I still fight over because we both believe that we made her up on our own.

Update: To date I have not written another song besides the love song to the fictional Laurie Pensive. Ella continues to assign the music video assignment, and the owner of the SK-10 has not responded to even one of my e-mail messages.

Tag # 000114
Final price: $9.50
Auction ended: Feb-14-01
Total bids: 10
Simi Valley, California

Ruby-Red Chrome Chair: Chairs in Iowa come cheap. I don't know whether I found this on the street or at the Crowded Closet. Either way I didn't pay more than a one dollar for it. It's a little beat up, but it does look nice in my kitchen next to my fifties-style chrome table. Although it is not my favorite chair in the kitchen, it is my second favorite. And although I don't read the paper sitting in this chair, I often eat my morning bowl of cereal in it.

Update: Cordelia bought my ruby-red chair early on in the project, but it took a while for us to figure out how to ship it. The first chair I sold cost more than forty dollars to ship, and as it turns out, Cordelia is a student, so paying that much for shipping didn't quite fit her budget. We came up with a compromise. I told her that I would try to ship the chair unwrapped and see whether or not my friends at the post office would take it. They were pretty used to me shipping strange items. They especially liked the time I shipped a sweet Vidalia onion. I addressed the chair to her friend Alex in Simi Valley and brought it to the post office. They sold me $16.50 worth of stamps and placed the chair in one of those canvas package carts. Alex wrote me to tell me that the chair had arrived safely and that the mail carrier had jokingly placed it under the welcome mat, like the smaller packages that they usually receive.

Robert Tillman's Pez Dispenser: EBay was created solely for the auctioning of Pez dispensers. Robert must have known this fact when he came to my inventory party with one little gift to donate to my eBay project. Such a know-it-all. I think I bought the Wonder Woman Pez with the thought of sending it to Bekah. I'm not sure why I never sent it to her, but Robert found the match and tagged them both. Tillman coined the word "minstallation" and has built a gallery dedicated to minstallation art in the bottom drawer of his desk, called the "Hardly Peppercorn" gallery. He recently sent out an international call for entries for minstallations in his gallery space.

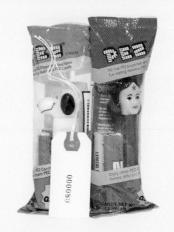

Tag # 000080
Final price: $2.00
Auction ended: Feb-14-01
Total bids: 4
Melbourne, Australia

Update: Alaina wrote me near the beginning of the sale and said that she thought this project would make an interesting book. We corresponded for a while and eventually she sent me a copy of a book that she had recently finished working on. Her book inspired me to work out a rough mock-up of what an allmylifeforsale book would look like. I showed that mock-up to my editor when I pitched this book to him last fall. I think that Alaina planned to buy both the smallest and the largest items that I listed. She was the high bidder on my Pez, as well as my oversize spinning seventies chair (page 125). I'm trying to get her to submit work to Robert's International Minstallation Exhibition.

Tag # 000123
Final price: $36.03
Auction ended: Feb-18-01
Total bids: 15
Brooklyn, New York

Opaque Projector: So I want to be able to tell you that I used this in a variety of different art installations at art museums around the world, but really that never happened. I bought it thinking that it could be a fun part of some installation or another. It is intended to display newspaper articles and the like on the wall. Me, I've never used it. I just really loved the box and wanted to rescue it from the thrift store. It's Italian, I think. Maybe you can use it to draw or paint with. Or maybe it will just sit in its box on your shelf, as it's done on mine.

Update: Miranda is an artist who lives and works in New York City. She was the first person I met through this project. It was awkward to go to a stranger's house in order to talk to them about something that they bought from me on eBay. Eventually, it became more or less routine for me, but I always remembered this first meeting and realize that the people I visited throughout this project probably felt the same way as I did on the day I met Miranda. We spoke for about twenty minutes and she showed me the new work she was making using my opaque projector. It was great to see that something from my life had affected its new owner. I'm still waiting to hear when Miranda's new work will be exhibited. I hope I will be invited to the opening.

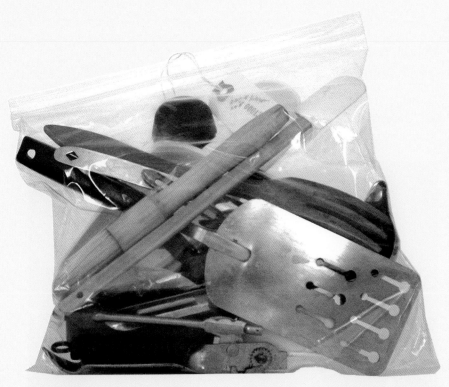

Tag # 000231
Final price: $2.75
Auction ended: Feb-25-01
Total bids: 4
Chicago, Illinois

Update: When this was up for auction I received a note from a woman who told me that I would surely regret selling the spoon that my grandfather made. I may regret it someday, but I still have a digital reproduction of it on my computer. I guess I won't be able to stir my grandfather's spaghetti recipe with it, but I still remember the recipe.

Bag of Kitchen Stuff: Everything that any kitchen would need. In fact, I have needed a few of these items since they were inventoried in October. It's hard to BBQ chicken without a basting brush. One of the wooden spoons in this bag was handmade by my grandfather William McGrath, God rest his soul. What is a kitchen without a can opener? I had a hard time opening my pork and beans yesterday. I need a new can opener for sure.

Update: Brian was wearing this shirt when I met up with him in Dallas this fall. He bought a few different things from me, including the half roll of toilet paper that someone tagged at my inventory party. We met for one drink in an overly hip section of Dallas and then went for some food in a less pretentious area by the Texas State Fair Grounds—the fair had ended the week before. Brian gave me a book of his poetry that he had self-published.

Tag # 000339
Final price: $13.50
Auction ended: Feb-18-01
Total number of bids: 17
Dallas, Texas

Empire Brewing Co. "Elvis" Shirt:
There were only ten of these shirts made at the Empire Brewing Company when they first opened. My cousin was a manager there and when I first moved to Syracuse, he found me a job as a busboy—a busboy with a B.A. Once in a while I would see people I went to college with and would have to bus their tables. So much for going to law school. It was fun though and eventually I started waiting tables, which is where the money is. When I was leaving, Lynn, the general manager, snuck this shirt out of the storeroom for me. It has the name ELVIS embroidered on it and was originally made for one of the owner's ex-wives, whose nickname used to be "Elvis."

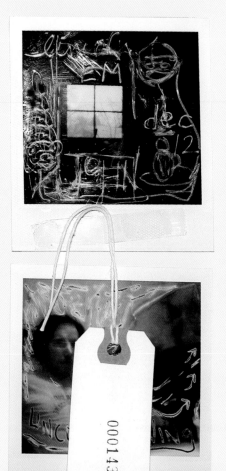

Two Polaroid Photographs: Two pictures taken in my kitchen with my Polaroid SX 70 camera. One photograph is of my kitchen window, the other is a picture of my friend Lincoln and me. The shutter speed was so slow that Lincoln looks ghostlike. Scratches in the emulsion of the image spell out "Lincoln leaving." Lincoln now lives in Denver, Colorado, and this photograph was taken the last time that I saw him before he left.

I have only been sick from drinking three times in my life. Once was when I was fourteen. Mark Galucci and Colin Flinn slept over at my house and we drank a bottle of my dad's gin. Then we got up at seven A.M. and hitched a ride from my dad to go skateboarding in Albany. About a block from my dad's office, I threw up all over my lap. The other two times both occurred after drinking with Lincoln.

Tag # 000143
Final price: $5.50
Auction ended: Mar-04-01
Total bids: 6
Iowa City, Iowa

Update: Jacob sent me a Polaroid of himself in front of my Polaroids. I visited Lincoln in Denver last fall and I am happy to report that I do not have an additional alcohol-poisoning story to add to the three mentioned. However, I cannot say that my three months on the road were devoid of such stories. When I visited Christine in Denton, Texas, we stopped at a local bar for a few drinks and I simply kept up with her drink for drink. I think that she may be related to Lincoln, because in the morning she was up at eight A.M. and I spent the next five hours between the couch and the bathroom making the familiar never-again promises to myself.

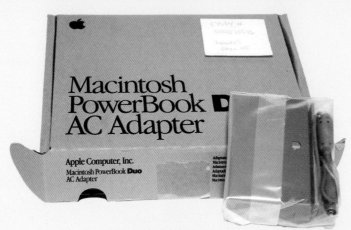

Tag # 000126
Final price: $26.99
Auction ended: Feb-22-01
Total bids: 8
London, United Kingdom

AC Power Adapter for PowerBook Duo: This is the second thing I ever bought on eBay; the first was also an AC power adapter for a PowerBook Duo. See, my first eBay experience was last spring after I had just found a used PowerBook at UI Surplus. It did not have a power adapter and the battery doesn't hold a charge, so I looked for a power supply on eBay. A new one from Apple would cost $120, so I was willing to pay a few dollars. I found one with a starting bid of six dollars. So I registered with eBay and started bidding. After five days of gradual bid increases I went to class feeling assured that my high bid of $12.32 would carry the auction later that day. I got sniped in the last minutes and lost the item by fifty cents. So I immediately went back to eBay and bid fifteen dollars on three separate AC power adapters for my little PowerBook. Five days later I was the proud owner of all three. This one is fresh out of the box. I received the other two first, so I've never used this one.

Update: For someone who sold everything he owns on eBay, you'd think that I'd replace everything via eBay too. But, to be honest, I have not bought a single thing on eBay since I bought the laptop that I am writing on. Sasha buys things every week—16 mm films, soap dishes, Jack Kemp light switch covers. I guess I'm afraid that if I went back to buying on eBay, within a year I'd have her house filled with three or four identical copies of everything I wanted. I'm not good at losing auctions.

PowerBook Duo 250: I bought this computer at UI Surplus. It was so clean and worked. I started to use it to do my e-mail on and to keep a somewhat daily journal. I brought this little guy with me when I lived in New York over the summer. For the first week or so before I found work with Sesame Workshop, I kept a fairly regular journal writing about hanging out in New York with my closest friends. It has a 14.4 modem, a pretty big hard drive for its time, and a black-and-white screen. It is one of the smallest PowerBooks ever made.

Update: The new owner confessed that she was more interested in reading the New York journal than in the computer itself. I think she may have been disappointed. I was terrible at keeping a journal, and "somewhat daily" was a generous use of language. Over the summer and fall I became much better at writing every day, but even then Temporama readers will remember that I went whole weeks without posting updates.

Tag # 000124
Final price: $102.50
Auction ended: Feb-25-01
Total bids: 36
Hammond, Indiana

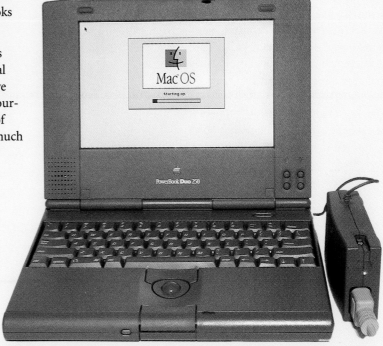

Tag # 000122
Final price: $10.50
Auction ended: Feb-22-01
Total bids: 12
Malvern, Pennsylvania

Milliampere Meter: So I have a problem. Why the hell do I own a milliampere meter? And why would you want one? I don't even know what a milliampere is. But at UI Surplus they sell all kinds of weird medical equipment, including devices used for shock-therapy experiments. I wonder if the energy used in shock therapy is measured in milliamperes. Please don't use this for any type of therapy. It looks damn cool though.

Update: Over the last year I received five or six messages explaining what a milliampere meter measures. I'm not sure what Robert is using it for, but I did find a science experiment on the Web where a hamster's wheel was hooked up to a meter like this to measure the amount of energy that it could generate. Will we soon hear an interview on NPR from Malvern, Pennsylvania, where a new source of alternative energy has been discovered?

Weston Meter: What should be done with a broken Weston meter? I have it sitting on a shelf in my house. It used to be in the glass table that I made out of a random shelf unit that Lanethea carried around with her. When she was the program director at WHCL at Hamilton College she asked the college wood shop to design and build new record racks for their amazing collection of jazz and blues records. The first shelf unit built had shelves that were thirteen-by-forty-two-by-six inches deep, not deep enough for a twelve-inch record. Well, that first rack became a glass table that we had in our apartment in Syracuse. That was a hard thing to leave behind, because it was a great place to display all of my old crap like this broken Weston meter. I'm not sure if they ever built the proper-size record racks, because a program director after Lanethea had the "brilliant" idea of turning WHCL radio "all digital", a great line on his résumé. That idiot disposed of the most amazing collection of vinyl that I have ever seen. I hope the radio station that eventually hired him appreciates the disservice that he did to the quality of radio in upstate New York.

Tag # 000401
Final price: $3.75
Auction ended: Feb-25-01
Total bids: 7
Castro Valley, CA

Update: Kevin wrote to tell me that the broken Weston meter that he bought from me is still broken. And Lanethea wrote me a brief e-mail asking my to remove her name from my Web site, because Google searches for her name turned up listings from allmylifeforsale instead of the journal articles that she authored and the conferences that she attended.

Tag # 000107
Final price: $16.50
Auction ended: Feb-25-01
Total bids: 17
Philadelphia, Pennsylvania

Pierce Trucking Hat: Well-worn, broken-in red-and-white PIERCE hat. This hat was brand new when I received it as a going-away gift from the students who worked with me at Light Work. It has traveled with me more than one-hundred-thousand miles, including a trip to Sweden and Norway. There is a little pin on the hat that I received as a gift from Johan. The pin features a bikini-clad woman on skis. Johan, Kristin, Hakon, Mari, and the gang made sure that Kris and I had the most incredible time in Styrn, Norway. Just so you know, Swedish National Day is best spent in Norway while listening to a Bulgarian music group singing "Sweet Home Alabama".

Update: Melissa bought this hat with the intention of giving it back to me when I visited this fall. I wasn't sure what to do when she tried to give it back; I had just gone through the process of selling everything that I owned and three weeks later this was offered back. I ended up wearing it around Philadelphia as a test run and within minutes I decided that if she didn't want the hat I could take it back, so much for freedom from possessions. When we visited the Philadelphia Museum of Art we ran into the fifty contestants from the Miss America Pageant, and Melissa and I tracked down Miss Iowa for a photograph.

普及版
COLLECTION
資料|マーク|シンボル|ロゴタイプ|1978→'79|
TRADEMARKS & SYMBOL MARKS
1978-'79 IN JAPAN
[編著]
長谷川純雄+
小林茂二
グラフィック社
'78→'79

000163

Tag # 000163
Final price: $25.00
Auction ended: Feb-25-01
Total bids: 29
Tyne & Wear, UK

Japanese Design Book: Hmm, I wonder if I should tell you who this is from. If you know anything about me by now you should be able to figure it out. This book is filled with various icons from Japanese design firms of the late 1970s. Icons, logos, fonts for hundreds of Japanese businesses. It is one of my favorite books (not a lot to read). If you are into design at all, this book emphasizes the clean and simple designs of the Japanese school.

Update: Susan's father gave her my Japanese design book as a gift. A number of people have offered to buy my book from her, but she tells them that the book is part of her project "my life not for sale". She studied design in college and has my book in a place of pride on her bookshelf. I wonder if she will look up one of the pages that I marked?

Tag # 000245
Final price: $22.00
Auction ended: Feb-18-01
Total bids: 10
Melbourne, Australia

8 mm Film Viewer: This is a book. Or at least that's what I called it when I ran old typewriter ribbon through it as a way to read the last words written on an old typewriter. I will include a long strand of unread typewriter ribbon. I'm not sure whether the ribbon contains latent love letters or old college papers, but chances are it includes both. I believe in a very loose definition of what constitutes a book.

Update: I guess Alaina believes that books can take many shapes too. I sent the 8 mm film viewer via surface mail sometime in March. The guy at the post office said that it might take more than six months to arrive. Maybe she thinks it is with the unsent spinning chair (page 125) still in storage in the basement of the UI art building.

Tag # 000039
Final price: $20.55
Auction ended: Mar-24-01
Total bids: 21
Omaha, Nebraska

Update: In February, Ben sent me a note telling me that he wanted to buy my least wanted items. I told him that I actually wanted all of the things that I was getting rid of, but he further clarified that he wanted the things that nobody else wanted. And so for the next two months he would be the first to bid on everything that I listed. At one point he had bids out on twenty separate items. In the end he wound up with about twenty-five pieces of my life. The twenty-one bids on this key chain did not quite qualify it as an unwanted object, but I guess he really wanted it.

Talking Japanese Key Chain: Gary Hesse gave me this key chain upon his return from a photography convention in Japan. Gary was my boss at Light Work. I learned so much from him in the three years that I worked with him—from how to clean, maintain, and repair a Hope color processer to almost everything that I know about digital imaging. Working at Light Work was amazing because we were so understaffed that I had more responsibility than I ever imagined having almost as soon as I started. It was one of the best jobs I have ever had, and much of that was due to the support and knowledge that I gained from working with people like Jeff Hoone, Gary Hesse, and Marylee Hodgens. There is a button on the back of the key chain that makes it say, "Each-how to-will-a-ka so soo-chi-i." I don't know what that means.

Tag # 000957
Final price: $18.02
Auction ended: Apr-04-01
Total bids: 12
Omaha, Nebraska

Light Work Twenty-fifth-Anniversary Contact Sheet: Light Work is a nonprofit arts organization whose mission is to support artists who work in photography. They do this in a variety of ways, including their twenty-year "artists in residence" program, their annual Light Work regional grant, exhibitions in their gallery spaces, and especially their award-winning publication *Contact Sheet,* which features the work of all of the artists who participate in Light Work's programs. This is the twenty-fifth-anniversary catalog and includes examples of work by literally every single artist who ever participated in their programs. *Contact Sheet* is available by subscription and in your local bookstore. There are no advertisements in *Contact Sheet,* so don't worry, you never have to be distracted by ads for Absolut vodka while you are trying to appreciate challenging work by emerging artists.

Tag # 000675
Final price: $2.50
Auction ended: Mar-10-01
Total bids: 4
Omaha, Nebraska

Brown Leather Belt: It's a belt. I'm a thirty-six waist or so. I remember "The Belt" from my childhood. I didn't see it that often, but on that rare occasion when you were really, really bad my father was the quickest belt remover on the planet. You would hear the jiggle of the buckle and two seconds later you'd be getting that belt slapped across your butt. Well, it certainly made an impression on me. I'm not sure if I'd ever use the belt on my own children when I have them, but I can't say that I didn't deserve what I got. I hope this belt doesn't see too much punishment action.

Update: I met Ben and his family last September when I drove through Omaha. They coined a new name for my project: "Operation Infinite Mooch." On the first night I was there I had dinner with Ben and his wife, Cindy. He arrived with my copy of the twenty-fifth-anniversary catalog. He was also wearing a T-shirt of a band that Sasha's friends are in. I stayed at their house one of the nights that I was in Omaha and met the rest of their family. Their daughter was wearing my belt, and had just washed and folded my Oklahoma tractor pullers shirt. It was just like I was in my own house.

Tag # 000402
Final price: $8.50
Auction ended: Mar-10-01
Total bids: 3
Omaha, Nebraska

Comic Books: I'm not alone in my collection of too much stuff. Last year at about this time I received a package from Bekah and Doug. It was filled with crap from their house that they didn't want anymore. So who did they send it to? Me, because half the crap they have in their house came from my massive pile of junk. Included in their pile of unwanted trash were these comic books. I never was into comic books. I like a good *Bazooka Joe* comic strip, but that is mostly due to the gum. Maybe the high bidder will do with them what Bekah, Doug, and I have not been able to bring ourselves to do and finally throw them out.

Update: I met Chris and his family this summer when I drove through Omaha. He too sees the potential in objects; he is a collector of sorts, and saves things in stacks around his house. I have started stacking again too; although I don't own much now. I mostly stack the junk mail that I continue to receive. When I visited he searched through his stuff looking for the comics that he bought from me. After fifteen minutes or so I decided to photograph him with another stack of comics that he found in the house. Maybe he took the above advice and threw them out.

Tag # 000235
Final price: $1.75
Auction ended: Mar-04-01
Total bids: 4
Omaha, Nebraska

Update: I think Ben's purchase of this was in keeping with his goal of trying to buy things from my project that nobody else wanted.

Weird Stuffed Bean Animal: I'm not sure if this has any of the collector value of, say, a Beanie Baby, but it is stuffed with some sort of puffy beans. I won this at Coney Island this summer. "Everybody wins, guaranteed prize," announced the barker to Maya and me. During my freshman year in college Maya and I were pretty much inseparable. When she met me I was a booster for the Catholic Church and she claims that I was even anti-choice, which I don't quite remember, but I hope not. (Now I'm an atheist, thanks in part to late-night chats with Maya.) Either way I got to hang out with her quite a bit this summer in New York City and she paid five dollars to the lady with the darts for our "Prize Every Time" and won this. It looks nothing like the prizes hanging over the darts; this one comes from a box behind the counter.

Tag # 000259
Final price: $26.50
Auction ended: Apr-04-01
Total bids: 18
Gainesville, Florida

Update: I placed the mailbag into an oversize shipping box and sent it to Florida. Although Kelly has never sent me an official update, after doing a Google search for "allmylifeforsale", I did find a link to a bulletin board exchange between her and a friend. She said that she wanted the bag as a way to support what I was doing. I never met her to thank her for that support.

Light Work Mail, 1972–1985: The best job at Light Work's Community Darkrooms was posting the art listings on the three oversize bulletin boards. It seemed like every arts organization in the world had Light Work's address and would send us notices of all of their upcoming events. The person who kept track of the bulletin boards was the most informed about the goings-on in the art world. They knew of every call for entries, every solo show, and even the popular trends in sculpture and painting. Well, for years Jeff Hoone saved every announcement that came into Light Work, announcements of shows by every major photographer in the seventies and early eighties, the likes of Nicholas Nixon, Bea Nettles, and Charles Gatewood. One day when I was cleaning out our storage space, I was asked to throw away all of this leftover mail, which had started to take up a huge portion of our limited space. I couldn't bear to see all of it go to the trash, so I filled a mailbag with handfuls of mail from the random boxes of archived mailings. So who wants a record of contemporary art as it appeared on Light Work's bulletin board over more than twenty years?

Tag # 000674
Final price: $2.50
Auction ended: Mar-21-01
Total bids: 4
Lynnwood, Washington

Update: I put Sandy's address on the outside of this plastic bag and brought it to my friends at the post office. A few weeks later I received a set of photographs showing the Lynnwood, Washington, squirrel population enjoying my bag of Iowa corn. My relationship with corn has changed so much since I arrived here. I used to think that it was funny to live in a state with so much corn, but I recently read that the chemical runoff from Iowa farms is a leading source of ocean pollution. Ocean pollution! We are a few thousand miles from any ocean.

Iowa Corn (Squirrel Corn): Each year I am surrounded by 6.2 million ears of corn. So, you might ask, why I would want to have any more? Well, I thought that I might do a little U.S. Postal Service experiment and see if I could just stick postage on ears of corn and send them to my friends. As with many of my ideas, this one never quite made it to the post office, but here is another opportunity. Now I can mail them to you, one at a time or in this nice plastic bag. I wouldn't recommend popping this stuff. But they feed it to the squirrels out here.

Update: I used to wear Robin's ring on my left middle finger; I think that people used to think I was married. The hairs on my finger haven't grown back yet and the slight indentation from five years of wear is still there, as if I just forgot to put it on today. When I went to visit Emily in Ohio, she tried to give it back to me. It was early in my travels and I was afraid that if I took it, soon my car would be filled with all the things that I had spent the last year selling. I think that if she offered it to me today I would put it on my finger and never take it off again.

Tag # 000008
Final price: $38.25
Auction ended: Mar-11-00
Total bids: 23
Columbus, Ohio

Silver Ring: This is the only ring that I have ever worn. My friend Robin gave me this ring about five years ago. I have worn it nearly every day since. I'm not one who normally wears rings, but Robin is one of my best friends and it was always nice to look down and have a little reminder of her. She lives in New York City, working to keep nonviolent offenders out of jail. She is saving the world and anyone who wears this ring will have a piece of the world that she is saving. I think the ring came from a trip she took to Mexico with her pharmaceutical-company-employee exboyfriend. What was his name again?

My Sideburns: At my inventory party some people thought that they would use the opportunity to challenge my resolve to go through with this project. Sara Langworthy tagged things that she knew would be near and dear to my heart: my cast-iron skillet, my turntable, a bottle of Maker's Mark. My friend Sasha tagged things that she didn't like. She tied a tag to my sideburns and explained how "late nineties" they were. And at some point a group of us went into the bathroom and clipped them off. Up until that day I had always had sideburns. I walked around for about two months feeling naked before I tried to grow a beard. No matter how long I let it grow it always looked like I was trying to grow a beard. I shaved my sad attempt at a beard and now I have sideburns again, but this time they are longer and fuller, more like Elvis in the seventies, less like a character on *90210*.

Update: I received an e-mail from the high bidder on my sideburns, who said that he had grand plans for his new purchase. For a while I was a little worried that he was a genetic engineer at Carnegie Mellon, and that his grand plan was to include my sideburns in a cloning experiment. A month later I received another e-mail from him saying that he no longer wanted to participate in my project. He decided to withdraw after he brought a copy of the *USA Today* article about my project and the Ziploc bag containing my sideburns to the head curator at the Pittsburgh Museum of Art. They refused to take the donations, and deemed the Ziploc bag and the project from which it came "Not Art!" I wonder if they will sell this book in their museum shop?

Tag # 000017
Final price: $19.50
Auction ended: Mar-18-01
Total bids: 19
Pittsburgh, Pennsylvania

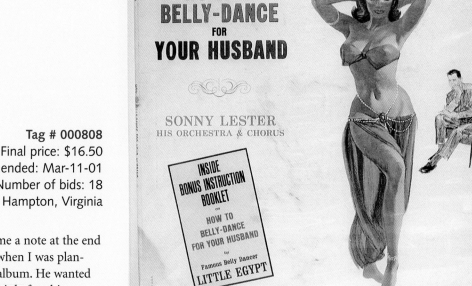

Tag # 000808
Final price: $16.50
Auction ended: Mar-11-01
Number of bids: 18
Hampton, Virginia

Update: Sean sent me a note at the end of February asking when I was planning on listing this album. He wanted to make sure I listed it before his September wedding, because he planned on having it framed and giving it to his wife at their rehearsal dinner. He invited me to the wedding, but I missed it. He said his wife is getting pretty good at belly dancing.

How to Belly Dance for Your Husband: This is the most requested item to go up for auction. Does every husband fantasize about having his wife dance for him? Me, I'm not married, so I guess I don't really need this, and besides, I already know how to belly dance. I snuck a peek or two at the instruction booklet, so I too could belly dance for my husband—even though I'm more likely to have a wife. It's pretty easy to learn. Almost like aerobics except for the sheer fabrics. I made a thirty-inch poster of this record cover. It was up on the wall at Bekah's for a little while. I wonder where it is now.

Tag # 000512
Final price: $90.00
Auction ended: Mar-10-01
Total bids: 18
Dallas, Texas

Good Old Gold Shirt: I received this shirt as a tip, from Matt at the Motley Cow Café in Iowa City. I used to wait tables there all last year. It was the best restaurant that I have ever worked in. It's really small, six tables or so, and really affordable. Tom uses organic vegetables when they are available and serves a few different specials every night of the week. On the first night that we started serving fresh fish (Tom was a vegetarian at the time), we accidentally sent out a piece of fish that needed some extra time, so to speak. Thank God it went to our most regular of regulars, the owners of Running Wild. The place was packed and just as we were about to send out the properly recooked fish, a tray fell to the ground, causing Joe and Jean to have to wait even longer to eat. Joe and Jean left me a fifty-dollar tip that night even though everything seemed to have gone wrong. Tom, Tito, and I went next door to Dirty John's Grocery and bought a fifty-dollar bottle of wine to share as we cleaned up for the night. If you are ever in Iowa City you will probably get a free drink or two if you show up wearing this shirt.

Update: Susan Kae Grant was the high bidder on this shirt when I performed a live auction last march at the Society of Photographic Education conference in Savannah, Georgia. She was in a fierce bidding war with other photographers John Pfahl, Margaret Stratton, and David Taylor. The proceeds of the auction went to the graduate scholarship fund. This year at the SPE conference in Las Vegas, Susan has asked me to reauction "Old Gold" to benefit that very same scholarship fund. The plan is to make the shirt auction an annual part of the scholarship fund-raiser. It should fetch a pretty good price this year in Vegas with all of the gold embroidery and rhinestone trim.

Tag # 000244
Final price: $66.00
Auction ended: Mar-10-01
Total bids: 13
London, United Kingdom

Iranian Bowling Shirt: This is my most coveted bowling shirt. When I go bowling, I always bring my collection of bowling shirts, and this shirt is always the first to go. Only the closest of the close have ever worn this shirt. Trey found it for me in some thrift store in San Francisco, and it is from "New Show Pizza" in Tehran, Iran. I wonder if there is still a pizza joint in Tehran. I wore this shirt when I invented "The Butt Dance" at some Skidmore College art opening. The dance includes a slow hip gyration with your butt out to the right side a little for two beats and then to the left side for one beat. Something may tell you that I'm sort of a dork....

Update: I talked to Trey today to see if he would read through the new text I have been working on for this book. He reminded me that about halfway through this project he really started to hate it. For a few months, talking to me was like having to read every page of my project twice: all my life, all the time. Also, as the project went on I started selling the things that I didn't really want to sell—the gifts that I received from friends and family, my cameras, and my books and catalogs. I guess I would hate a project where Trey sold off all the things that I ever gave him. I was wearing this shirt on the day that I went to the post office and received the English money order for the sixty-six-dollar bid.

Hamilton College Sweatshirt: Hamilton is a small liberal arts college in upstate New York, just outside of Utica. It has a strange mix of students. On one side there are public-school kids for which Hamilton was their top choice, and on the other there are prep-school kids who use Hamilton as a backup school in case they get rejected from the Ivy League. Which makes Hamilton both a place of academic rigor (which I attribute to my public-school brethren) and also one of the top-ten party schools according to *Rolling Stone* in the early nineties (which I attribute to folks who were rejected from Harvard, Brown, and Yale). I spent a good chunk of my time at Hamilton trying to eliminate the discriminatory practices of Hamilton College's fraternities, which were quite proud of their role in the top-ten party rating and a little less proud of their contribution to the drop of Hamilton out of the *U.S. News* top twenty.

Tag # 000513
Final price: Unknown
Auction ended: Mar-10-01
Total bids: Unknown
Destination: Unknown

Update: Everyone asks me where this sweatshirt ended up. I shipped so many things at the beginning of March that I couldn't even keep track of where everything went. A few times I sent the wrong item to the wrong person. I assume that this arrived safely at its destination, because I haven't received any negative feedback on eBay. Hamilton returned to the *U.S. News* top twenty this year.

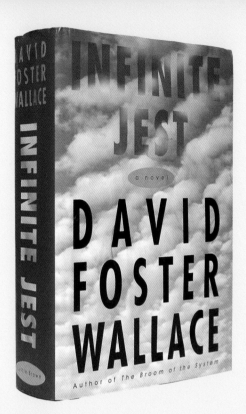

Tag # 000590
Final price: $7.50
Auction ended: Mar-21-01
Total bids: 9
Iowa City, Iowa

Update: Todd inventoried everything he owned for his graduate art thesis at the University of Iowa. Is there something in the water here? I wonder if he added my book to his inventory sheet. My sister Marnie still won't forgive me for selling her borrowed copy of this book. I received a bookstore gift certificate from her for Christmas this year and just ordered the paperback edition for her. I read *The Corrections* from cover to cover a month ago, so I know that I am capable of finishing a book. Maybe it was the book.

Infinite Jest, **One-Eighth Read:** Lanethea and my sister Marnie used to have a running joke about my reading habits or lack thereof. The joke would go, "John, have you ever read [insert best-selling book by best-selling author]?" And my response would be: "You know, you could save yourself a few syllables if you just asked me 'Have you ever read?' because the answer will be the same. 'No.'" Well, I borrowed this book from Marnie three years ago this month and it is still far from read. It did, however, travel with me everywhere I've been, including Utah, Oregon, Vancouver, Sweden, Norway, California, New York City, Austin, Memphis, Atlanta, Mississippi, Las Vegas, and even Iowa City. All with the hopes of being read. Maybe you can read it and send it back to my sister when you are done. At least she would get it back then. It weighs slightly less than the *OED* that I sold last month.

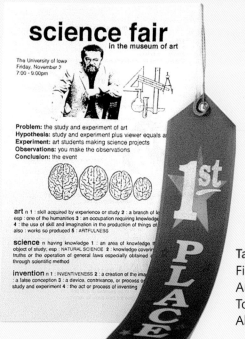

science fair
in the museum of art

The University of Iowa
Friday, November 3
7:00 - 9:00pm

Problem: the study and experiment of art
Hypothesis: study and experiment plus viewer equals a[...]
Experiment: art students making science projects
Observations: you make the observations
Conclusion: the event

art n 1 : skill acquired by experience or study 2 : a branch of l[...]
esp : one of the humanities 3 : an occupation requiring knowledge
4 : the use of skill and imagination in the production of things of [...]
also : works so produced 5 : ARTFULNESS

science n having knowledge 1 : an area of knowledge t[...]
object of study, esp : NATURAL SCIENCE 2 : knowledge coverin[...]
truths or the operation of general laws especially obtained a[...]
through scientific method

invention n 1 : INVENTIVENESS 2 : a creation of the ima[...]
: a false conception 3 : a device, contrivance, or process o[...]
study and experiment 4 : the act or process of inventing

Tag # 000248
Final price: $12.50
Auction ended: Mar-10-01
Total bids: 6
Albany, California

First-Place Ribbon: Last fall the art museum at the University of Iowa hosted a science fair and invited all of the art students to submit science projects. I decided to do an on-location experiment to answer the question "How Much Does a Pound Weigh?" So I went to the store and bought a pound-and-a-quarter sirloin steak, borrowed a friend's George Foreman Grill, and found an extension cord that could run from the grill to the electrical outlet directly below the museum's most prized possession, Peggy Guggenheim's Jackson Pollack. I cooked the steak to a perfect medium rare, and weighed myself before I sat down to one of the most satisfying meals I have ever had. Million-dollar paintings add such a fine-dining ambience to any meal. Well, it turns out that one pound actually equals three when consumed in front of famous paintings. Before the steak I weighed 177 pounds, and after eating the steak, unseasoned and with no beverages of any kind, I weighed 180 pounds. The science fair judge had seen similar experiments in the lab, but none had yielded such remarkable results. I attribute the gain in weight to the Miracle of the Jackson Pollock, but if you are the highest bidder on this item you can attribute it to anything you want.

Update: Shortly after I sent this to the woman in Albany, California, who also bought my unexposed rolls of film (page 137), I received a message from Donna. She wanted to know how to get in contact with the first-place ribbon's new owner. A few weeks later Kiem wrote me to tell me that she had resold my former prize to Donna at a considerable profit. So it has now returned to Iowa City. I never lost the three pounds that I put on that night, and the heart-stopping food that I ate on the road last year has added a few more pounds to the miracle three.

Tag # 000671
Final price: $27.00
Auction ended: Mar-21-01
Total bids: 10
Bangor, Maine

Update: I met up with Michael Mandiberg last summer when I visited a few of the high bidders in New York City. I tried to convince him to join me in visiting Owen, the new owner of our book. By the time I came through New York again in the fall, Mandiberg had already left for graduate school in California, so we never made the road trip to Maine. Owen paid slightly less for the book than I did.

Five Thousand Artists Return, Book Purchased from Shop Mandiberg:
Michael Mandiberg is an artist who also put everything that he owned up for sale on the Internet. He made everything available for purchase, including his wallet, house keys, jars of jelly, crackers, and even his Brown diploma. Our projects started nearly simultaneously, mine in November and his the following January. A friend of mine sent me a link to his site because the idea was similar to what I was doing. He set up a catalog store and priced everything according to its value to him. His house keys were available for six thousand dollars, his wallet slightly more. I bought this copy of *Five Thousand Artists Return* because I wanted to support his project and because I think the Internet is starting to emerge as an alternative art space in much the same way that nonprofits like Artists Space began in the early seventies.

Jen's Art Videos: Last December I drove from Iowa City to Syracuse, New York, in eighteen hours, through some of the worst weather that I had ever seen. The trip, which normally takes fourteen hours, took so long because it took me four hours to drive the fifty miles of the New York State Thruway by Buffalo. I arrived five minutes before the start of the final screening for the video students in the Department of Art Media Studies at Syracuse University. I came to see the video that my friend Jen had been working on all semester long, called *Bat Mitzvah.* All for naught, because the person who organized the screening thought that Jen had accidentally handed him somebody's home video of their Bat Mitzvah, so instead I got to watch a bunch of glorified rock videos that tried to show "the perspective of heroin running through your veins". *Bat Mitzvah* documented Jen's neighbor's coming-of-age event from the perspective of someone who has always had video technology around her. You may remember Jen; she was the Huggies baby "Maggie the Magnificent" in the commercial that ran during the royal wedding of Charles and Diana. I don't think that *Bat Mitzvah* is on this tape, but her Long Island Rail Road video is.

Tag # 000562
Final price: $18.50
Auction ended: Apr-04-01
Total bids: 11
Orange Grove, Texas

Update: I guess I have become the distributor of Jen's work. Like many of the people who bought things from me, Jimmy never sent me an update on this item. When someone bought a utilitarian item like RAM or a laptop computer from me, I seldom expected him or her to keep me posted on the object. But when I sold artwork made by my friends, I thought that the new owners would at least let me know that it arrived safely and was in good hands. Maybe he was scared to death after he watched Jen's short video about square-dancing automobiles.

Tag # 000810
Final price: $14.69
Auction ended: Mar-24-01
Total bids: 11
New York, New York

Update: Jedidiah wrote me to complain about the condition of the record that I sent him. Now I will admit that many of my item descriptions fail to even mention the object that they describe, but this listing plainly stated that the record came from a barn in Wisconsin. I refunded his money in full and asked him to ship the record to its rightful owner, Bekah. She is happy to have it back.

The Ventures, *Walk Don't Run:* So I may get killed for selling this record. Bekah's grandparents live on a farm near Green Bay, Wisconsin, and one summer when she went to visit she found a bunch of old records in the barn, one of which was this slightly beat-up old Ventures record. It doesn't skip, but it was in a hot and then cold barn for twenty years or so, far from the record archive at your local public library. This record was the first surf-guitar rock that I ever listened to, and I soon became addicted. My mix tapes changed dramatically when I got into surf rock. My tapes would go from serious disco to "The House of the Rising Sun" and back to jazz, hardly a list of floor fillers.

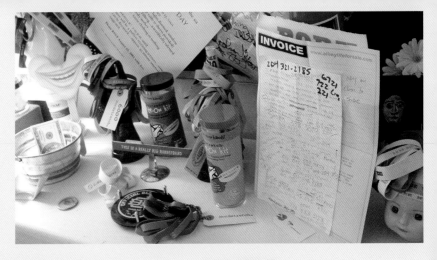

Telephone List: Handwritten telephone list of friends and businesses in Iowa City. When I moved to Iowa City I only knew two people: Margaret Stratton, who teaches at the University of Iowa, and Thomas Comerford, who I went to college with. Thomas gave me this sheet of paper with the names and phone numbers for various people who might be interested in the type of work I make. I now work as a research assistant for Ebon Fisher, whose name is at the top of the list; I have taken a few classes with Franklin Miller, who is the next name down; and the last name is my friend Kent, who ran the Thaw Festival in Iowa City. The rest of the names and numbers are my additions. Some folks I still speak to, some I don't.

Update: When I visited the Twin Cities this summer, I called all the people in the area who bought things from me, and at one point I called Ave Green, who I imagined as the long-lost brother of Al Green, a tall, deep-voiced African American man. So it was a bit of a surprise when Ave Maria Green answered her phone. She had my list on display in her office, and while I was there I tried to convince her to call the direct line of the executive producer of *Good Morning America*, whose number I had scribbled down in March when they broadcast from my house. She hasn't called him yet.

Tag # 000012
Final price: $14.50
Auction ended: Apr-01-01
Total bids: 13
St. Paul, Minnesota

Ray Charles, *Modern Sounds in Country and Western Music:* After another of my failed relationships, I moved into the house of "Uncle Ted", as my friend Mark called him. Uncle Ted is a professional painter at Syracuse University. He was divorced and had a huge house that was basically empty except for his room and the kitchen on the first floor. Mark called him "Ted" after Ted Nugent, because he fancied himself quite a sportsman and would fish and hunt nearly every single day. Seriously. He ice-fished all winter long.

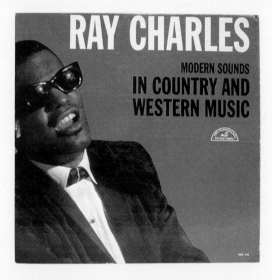

And when he would come home after a few hot toddies on the ice, he would turn his stereo on as loud as it would go and blast Hank Williams tunes on repeat. Needless to say it drove me crazy, and within six months I quit my job and moved to Salt Lake City. And while I was out there I vowed never listen to another Hank Williams song again—until I found this record. I think that I should just send it to Uncle Ted.

Tag # 000817
Final price: $27.00
Auction ended: Mar-21-01
Total bids: 16
Madison, Wisconsin

Update: Last week I was in my friend Mark's consignment shop and found this record in the music section. I haven't bought it yet. I'm still trying to avoid the inevitable reaccumulation of objects. How long will it take for me to fill up the house that I live in? Gelsy teaches at the University of Iowa and she was a little disappointed when I gave her the record because the color didn't match the picture that I listed on eBay. I guess I should just make her a print of the photograph and ask for the record back

Tag # 000853
Final price: $21.50
Auction ended: Apr-04-01
Total bids: 15
Newark, Texas

Update: Keith has my former sweater on display in his auto-supply shop in Newark, Texas. I have added his shop to the group exhibition listing on my résumé, right under the Museum of Modern Art. I tried to stop in and see him when I was last in Texas, but I couldn't find Newark on the map.

My Girlfriends' Favorite Sweater: When I was sixteen my mother's high-school friend Jackie Tolles opened a Benetton store in Saratoga Springs. I applied for a job there because I was getting a little tired of working at Kyer's Stables, where I had shoveled manure since I was fourteen. The Benetton policy was that the employees had to wear Benetton clothing during work hours. But I couldn't afford to buy the overpriced clothes (even with my discount), so they let me just put on a sweater off the rack for my shift. I would always come into work after skateboarding all over town, so I was usually quite sweaty. I would like to take this opportunity to apologize to all of the people who paid too high a price for a sweater that may or may not have been worn by a very sweaty and probably dirty skateboarder during the years of 1987–1989. I hope you had your sweater professionally dry-cleaned before you wore it out. (If not, I would recommend you dry-clean your Benetton sweater immediately.) Oh, as for this sweater, Jackie Tolles gave it to me for my birthday, and every girlfriend I have ever had loved this sweater.

Tag # 000781
Final price: $20.50
Auction ended: Apr-19-01
Total bids: 13
Honolulu, Hawaii

Webster Portable Typewriter: I have used this typewriter to fill in my tax forms. It's always good to have one around. I bought this at the Crowded Closet in Iowa City and I imagined that it was previously owned by one of the writers from the Iowa Writers' Workshop. Who knows, maybe it was owned by a farmer who did his taxes on it. It's a nice little typewriter.

Update: It costs the same to ship a typewriter to Kalona, Iowa, as it does to Honolulu. Maybe that is why the post office operated at a loss last year. The high bidder sent me a pound of Kona coffee in exchange for the cost of shipping. I tried to finish the beans before I sold my French press coffeepot.

Tag # 000120
Final price: $36.00
Auction ended: Mar-24-01
Total bids: 12
Indiana, Pennsylvania

Wire Camera Sculpture: Saori Hoshi made this sculpture for me seven years ago. It is made out of wire screen, and has a spool of fiberglass mesh that acts as a roll of film. Saori will certainly be famous someday. This is one of those things that I have carried with me wherever I go. It reminds me that I am a photographer and that Saori is my friend.

Update: I didn't make it to Indiana, Pennsylvania, but I am confident that the new owner of Saori's camera is taking good care of it. Actually I have found that much of what I've sold has ended up in better homes than where it came from. Stuff that I used to have crowded into boxes and piles is now displayed with pride in people's homes, all with a new history to explain to visitors.

Tag # 000958
Final price: $20.50
Auction ended: Apr-04-01
Total bids: 25
London, United Kingdom

Al and Irene's BBQ T-Shirt: When I moved here the first thing that I asked about was BBQ. In Syracuse there is the best BBQ that I have ever had from the Dinosaur BBQ, so I missed home and was in search of a substitute. Well, Al and Irene's BBQ in Cedar Rapids is no substitute for the Dinosaur, because it is in its own class of BBQ. Al makes everything from scratch. Everything! There is no canned anything in his pantry. All his beans are dried and soaked, all his sauces are made from scratch, all his french fries are fresh cut.

Update: Dave wrote me to tell me that my yellow shirt is now one of his favorites. He works with Steve, who bought my brick last March (page 78). They work for the same firm, which did the computer animation for movies like *Tomb Raider* and *Gladiator*. Both he and Steve invited me to visit them in London if I ever make it over there. Dave says he wants to come to Iowa and sample some Al and Irene's BBQ. I guess he's invited if he wants to visit. Does this mean that I have to invite all of the high bidders to visit me in Iowa?

Tag # 001003
Final price: $1.00
Auction ended: Apr-27-01
Total bids: 1
Tokyo, Japan

Update: Alaina bought these for her parents in Japan. I packed them in an oversize box with lots of bubble wrap and sent them via airmail. I used to send packages to Japan fairly regularly when Saori lived there. She just moved back this year, so it looks like I will be shipping stuff there once again.

Porky's BBQ Pork Skins: This is one of those things that I bought solely based on the packaging. I'm not sure that I've ever tasted pork skins. Now, it's not that I'm afraid of eating fried pork, I'm quite a fan of pork. The Dinosaur BBQ in Syracuse has a menu item that is simply named "fired pork hunks", one of my favorite food items there. I also heard that pork rinds were George Bush Sr.'s favorite snack.

Tag # 000531
Final price: $10.50
Auction ended: Apr-19-01
Total bids: 11
Claremont, California

Latham Homes T-shirt: My dad is a retired attorney, a lifelong Republican who voted for none other than Ralph Nader. I almost voted for Gore until I heard who my dad had voted for. I couldn't have my dad voting left of me. Why would a lifelong Republican vote for Nader? Well, I have a few ideas: as an attorney he got to watch his corporate clients actively pollute the environment, defraud the government, and lay off American workers. One day I bought this mobile-home-manufacturing shirt at a thrift store. The first time that I wore this at home my dad asked me where I had gotten it. He had represented Latham Homes in court.

Update: Katherine is in the Claremont Divinity School, and she bought my Latham Homes T-shirt from me. She explained that she bought my shirt to use as an example in an upcoming Sunday sermon. She said she saw parallels between what I was doing and what Christ had done; he got rid of all of his possessions and wandered the countryside too. I tried to explain to her that Christ gave the proceeds to the poor, while I have a laptop computer and a car and have given the money that I raised to Mobil, Amoco, and Exxon. Katherine believes that if you have faith in Christ your needs will be taken care of. That if you drive into L.A. without a place to stay, the calls you make will be answered; that food will be served when you arrive at a dinner party even if you're an hour late because of traffic. She said she would send me a copy of her sermon.

Retro Seventies Spinning Chair: When I moved to Iowa City, the only furniture I had was stuff that I could fit in my car. Which meant that I didn't have any. While staying at Margaret's house I started to collect stuff off the streets and at garage sales in the neighborhood. Her back porch started to fill up with the various things that I would find. I got this chair at one such garage sale. The family was selling this chair against the protests of their children, who spent most of the garage sale guarding their spinning friend. After I paid for the chair I had to get the dad to remove his kids from my new property so I could take it with me. They were not very happy about it. Nor will I be happy when I have to ship it to someone else. When people visit my house they tend to sit in this chair and within minutes they start to spin.

Update: Sadly, Alaina's chair is still in the basement of the art building at the University of Iowa. We discovered that it would cost more than three hundred dollars to ship the chair to Melbourne. She has written a grant to the Australian Arts Council requesting money to ship the chair. She wants to make a book of photographs featuring my old chair in front of all the Australian national landmarks.

Tag # 000384
Final price: $56.00
Auction ended: May-12-01
Total bids: 23
Melbourne, Australia

Tag # 000057
Final price: $24.99
Auction ended: Apr-19-01
Total bids: 12
Charlottesville, Virginia

Old Unknown Photographs: I bought a huge stack of photographs at the Syracuse flea market one Saturday. They are obviously from someone's family box of pictures. It is interesting to look at the children growing up and the girls' interaction with their father. These folks were well-to-do. It looks like they spent a fair amount of time in Florida in the thirties and time in the Adirondack Mountains in the summers. I often throw one or two of the photos into letters that I write my friends. One day I was writing my friend Sara Gibbs in Utah when I came across a photograph of a farm in northern New York. The farm is on Route 28 near Gore Mountain, where Sara and I used to teach snowboarding. We had passed that run-down farm hundreds of times, and when I went to stuff a random image in the letter I wrote, I found the image of that farm.

Update: I haven't written a letter to Sara since the one that contained the old photograph, but I did get a chance to see her this fall in Utah. She didn't mention the photograph, but I'm sure she still has it somewhere. Phil bought the images and said he planned on scanning them and making them accessible on the Web. I haven't found them out there yet but will link to them when I do.

Sara Gibbs's Dad's Hat: Sara's dad is a great skier; he continues to ski every weekend of the season at Gore Mountain in upstate New York. Gore is where I met Sara. She is one of the toughest skiers I ever met, and when she decided to take up snowboarding she got even tougher. During her first weeks of learning to snowboard she tried to keep up with all of her speed-addicted (not the drug) ski buddies. She would just point her board down and attempt to keep up with people on race skis. And she did. It was crazy. Apart from having taken some of the nastiest spills I have ever seen, Sara is one of the fastest snowboarders I know. The last time I went riding with her at Snowbird (there are ten or so skiers and boarders from Gore Mountain who live and work in Utah now), I couldn't even keep up, and I have been snowboarding for fifteen years. Sara's family has always skied and used to have a virtual museum of bad ski fashions from the sixties through the eighties, and this hat was one such example.

Update: Now why would someone in London want a late-seventies ski hat? Does it really get that cold in the winter? Sara wasn't too happy when I sold her father's hat, but she was a little amused when I told her where it ended up. The only feedback that the new owner sent me was on eBay, where he said he was "pleased to be part of this art thing". I wonder if anyone in London recognizes the hat as mine.

Tag # 000780
Final price: $26.02
Auction ended: Apr-04-01
Total bids: 20
London, United Kingdom

127

Tag # 000945
Final price: $16.50
Auction ended: Apr-19-01
Total bids: 9
Dallas, Texas

Converse Sneakers: Last month Converse declared bankruptcy. In March they laid off all of their American and Mexican manufacturing workforce. This is what happens when you ask fairly paid American men and women to compete with thirteen-year-old children working in foreign sweatshops. So Converse All-Stars will now be manufactured in China. These are the last pair of American-made Converse that I will ever own. The new ones will be made in China, and even though they will now cost less than a dollar to make, they will still cost thirty-two dollars in the stores.

Update: The Chinese-made Converse went on sale last month at the local shoe store. They still come in the same red-white-and-blue boxes, still come in the same standard colors, and still cost about $32.00 a pair. My shoes went to Texas.

Tag # 000706
Final price: $128.50
Auction ended: Apr-19-01
Total bids: 22
Johnstown, New York

Wild Bill's Motorola Radio: Wild Bill's coffee shop is in North Hall at the University of Iowa. The place is filled with random items for sale to benefit a charity. Last week they had a 1968 AFM cruiser bicycle that I wish I could have bought. I'm trying not to buy any more stuff because this project has to end. Well, anyway, I bought the radio there a few months back and now I have to sell it. It's only AM, but in Iowa that is fine since our NPR news station, WSUI, is on AM 910. And when I lived in New York City this summer, I found that WNYC is on the AM band too. It's made of metal, so it will probably last forever.

Update: Lee collects radios and I think this one nearly completed his collection. But as a former collector, I know that nothing really completes a collection; there are always new things to add and broken things to fix. I haven't started collecting again since the sale ended. I'm not sure where I would start. Maybe I could start collecting small things. My friend Maya has a collection of garbage. Well, actually, it is a collection of photographs of garbage. I think that might be the best way to collect. Just photograph stuff and leave it where it is.

Update: A week after I sent the empty box to Chester Springs, I received a postcard from the Great Old Box. The new owner, Ashley, decided to take the box with her on a business trip to Boston and dropped me a postcard when they arrived. In the coming weeks I received postcards from up and down the East Coast and a month or so later I received one from Europe. Ashley carried the box around with her everywhere she flew and started to fill the empty box with souvenirs from every place she visited. I visited her this summer and we took the box bowling. Her plan is to return the box to me when it is finally filled. Because of increased security, the airlines wouldn't allow her to carry the Great Old Box on the plane, so the postcards stopped for a while. But I just received word from Pittsburgh, so they seem to be on the move again.

Tag # 001030
Final price: $20.50
Auction ended: Apr-27-01
Total bids: 12
Chester Springs, Pennsylvania

Great Old Empty Box: This is a great box. Like much of what I own, I got this box at UI Surplus. Joe had a few thousand of these boxes and would give them out with every purchase. At one point I had ten or twelve of them. Trey has one that he cut down to fit in a movie that he worked on. I used this one as a portfolio box when I applied to the UI Center for the Book. It's rather beat up but has a nice "patina" of stamps and such. They no longer have any of these boxes at Surplus. I have since used the rest of these boxes to ship stuff out. What would you ship in such a beat-up box?

Pork Pantry Leftover: What exactly is "mechanically separated chicken"? My friend Mark always envisioned a chicken-farm robot that would chase the chickens around the yard when they tried to congregate. All of his other explanations made meat products with mechanically separated ingredients pretty hard to eat. Somebody brought this can of Vienna sausages to my Pork Pantry Potluck Party last spring. I wonder how long it was in their pantry before they brought it to my house. It's been in mine for a year now and I have no plans of popping the top and having a little meat snack. I'd prefer to think about the little robot in the chicken yard.

Tag # 000549
Final price: $2.25
Auction ended: Jun-08-01
Total bids: 4
Chester Springs, Pennsylvania

Update: Mike lives with Ashley. They met five years ago in an online chat room and have lived with each other in three different cities for the last few years. Mike works for a dot-com-style company and has been fortunate enough not to be laid off yet. Mike bought just about any food-related item that I listed, from my Vidalia onion to the cryptic chrysanthemum beverage, which was also left over from my pantry party. Mike and Ashley plan to release my Vienna sausages into their natural habitat. They are looking for a local supermarket that carries the same brand, so they can release it on the right shelf. Watch out for mechanically separated chicken in your local market.

Tag # 000341
Final price: $10.50
Auction ended: Jun-08-01
Total bids: 8
Chester Springs, Pennsylvania

Road Trip Recording: In February of 1999, I went on a road trip with Trey through a good chunk of the South. We drove through Memphis, Nashville, New Orleans, and Galveston, ending up in Austin, Texas. Along the way I made recordings. Sometimes I would just hang the microphone in the car and record what was said. It seemed like I always had the thing recording. I recorded our unguided tour of Graceland, the first parade of Mardi Gras, and countless miles of road noise. "Thump, thump … shhhhhhhhh…. Thump, thump … shhhhhhhh … Thump, thump…." I have no idea what is on this tape.

Update: I ended up sending Ashley, who bought the Great Old Empty Box (page 130), a couple of the tapes from that trip.

Tag # 000707
Final price: $10.50
Auction ended: May-12-01
Total bids: 6
Chester Springs, Pennsylvania

Update: Mike let me wear this shirt when we took the Great Old Box bowling (page 130).

City Café Bowling Shirt: The Edlunds gave me this shirt when Kris Ostness and I were staying with them after our lease ran out in Salt Lake City. The Edlunds are my family in Utah, and I'm not alone. They take in all kinds of strays, like Kris, Bill Stevenson, and Krissi too. Whenever any of us needs a place to stay, the door is always open and the kitchen is open late. Kris and I would never have been able to complete a single film had it not been for the generosity of the Edlunds. I'm not sure whether or not this is an authentic bowling shirt. It looks a little new to me, and it's 100 percent cotton. Real bowlers would never be caught in anything but polyester. But I have bowled in this shirt a few times and it's helped my score stay high. I'm not sure how I will ever keep my scores up when I no longer own a bowling shirt.

Tag # 000925
Final price: $5.00
Auction ended: Apr-27-01
Total bids: 4
Madison, Wisconsin

Update: Is it possible not to shop at Wal-Mart? Since I wrote that last year I think I have gone to Wal-Mart once. I was in Lubbock, Texas, on a Sunday morning and needed to get an oil change before I got on the road again. On a Sunday Wal-Mart is the only place open for business in Texas– it's the day of rest, you know. On the road somewhere I realized that if you shift the dash over, Wal-Mart becomes Walm-Art. After this discovery I spent the next eight hours or so trying to come up with what the "Walm" could stand for in a new art project that I was imagining. Three months in the car often leads to this type of thinking.

Dickies Jeans, Well Worn: I wear these pants nearly every single day. Last year I went to the doctor to get a physical, and he asked me how often I wore the pants that I was wearing. I told him that I wore them nearly every single day and he instructed me to get a couple of pairs. Well, I did, and these are the second of three pairs of Dickies that will go up for auction. They are really good jeans and only cost $17.50 a pair at stores around here. I bought these at Wal-Mart. Last spring I worked as a production assistant on a commercial for Wal-Mart. A week or so after I worked on the job, I was listening to an interview on NPR about an ad that Wal-Mart ran that featured women in a factory thanking Wal-Mart for keeping them employed by buying American-made goods. The only trouble is that by the time the ad had actually aired, the featured women had been laid off because Wal-Mart had canceled their contract and given it to a Chinese company instead. I don't shop at Wal-Mart anymore.

Tag # 000511
Final price: $1.00
Auction ended: Jun-16-01
Total bids: 1
Madison, Wisconsin

Nasty Old Shirt: I have owned this shirt for more than ten years. I think I stole it from my brother Mark, which means it probably had a pretty hard life before I started wearing it every day. Do you ever get that way about old clothing? This was a top-of-the-pile shirt, a shirt that was always one of the first ones that I would wear after I did my laundry. It would end up being worn two or three times before I did the laundry again. Lanethea wanted to make this shirt into a rag on more than one occasion. Will you make rags out of one of my most worn shirts?

Update: Brandon is a student in Madison. I don't think he has made this shirt into rags yet. In the end he bought an entire John Freyer outfit on eBay. He owns this shirt and a similar blue one that I sent him when I couldn't find the original at first, as well as a pair of my jeans and my Dekalb Genetics hat. He sent me a photograph of himself in Norway with my jeans on. He was standing on the side of a mountain road by one of the fjords that I visited three years ago. I think I might have a picture of myself standing in the same spot where his photograph was taken.

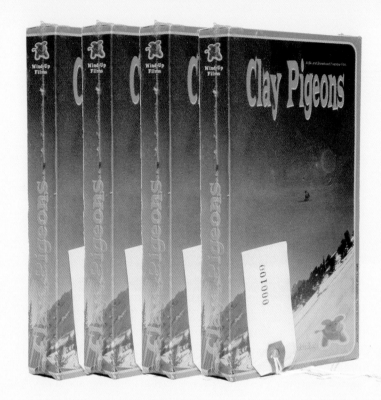

Tag # 000100
Final price: $10.50
Auction ended: Jun-16-01
Total bids: 5
Memphis, Tennessee

Update: Don is a fifty-one-year-old carpenter from Memphis and has started to pursue filmmaking on the side with consumer digital video equipment and a video-editing system that he set up on his computer. While most of the pieces that he's completed so far document the rich music culture of the Memphis community, in his last message to me he said that he was talking to four-wheeler-racing enthusiasts about making a mud-boarding film. I'm not even sure if there is such a thing as mud-boarding, but after Don documents it maybe we'll see a new Olympic sport for the Summer Games.

Clay Pigeons, **Ski/Snowboard Movie:** Not that bad movie with Janeane Garafalo. No, this movie is of a different sort. The title came from reviewing the footage with a friend, who said that the riders looked like skeet flying through the air. I left Light Work in February of 1999 to help Kris make the film we had always talked about making. We went to the ski industry trade show in Las Vegas with a two-minute trailer and somehow convinced a few sponsors to help us finish the film. We spent most of 1999 traveling from place to place shooting skiers and riders. We ended up filming in Sweden, Norway, Canada, and all over the United States, including Mount Hood in July. Last year Kris made *Tee Time* without me, and is working on Wind-Up Films' third film, *The Flying Circus*. Each year things get tighter and tighter, but I still love the first film. It's made with a shaky out-of-focus Super 8. Even my nonskiing friends love this film.

Tag # 000595
Final price: $26.01
Auction ended: May-02-01
Total bids: 10
Albany, California

Update: Kiem promptly processed my rolls of film when they arrived. She sent me copies of the contact sheets, which spanned a period of five or six years, from my ski trip to Sweden to my first year in Iowa. I'm not sure if she ever made prints from the photographs, but I think I might ask her if I can borrow them to make prints for myself in the future. Would that be cheating?

Five Unprocessed Rolls of 120 Film: It's the constant problem of any photographer. Always process your film as soon as you have shot it. If you don't it will end up in a drawer. When you move you will put the contents of that drawer into a box, and when you get there you'll empty that box into a new drawer. That has happened to me three or four times, which has rendered these rolls of film unidentifiable. So I can't promise the contents of any of these rolls of film. I know that I had a 120 camera when I was in college. I have also had a few Diana and Holga cameras in the last few years, so there could be photographs from just about anywhere I have been.

Handmade Twenty-five-Dollar Bills: The Secret
Service has two responsibilities. The most well known
one is guarding the president of the United States and
all his living predecessors. The Secret Service's other duty
is to protect U.S. currency from counterfeiting. Print shops
used to be frequently monitored to see whether or not illegal
money was being printed. The University of Iowa Printmaking
Program is number one in the nation, and last year, if the Secret Service
snooped around, they would have discovered a group of printmakers
who invented a new denomination of U.S. currency: the twenty-five-dollar
bill. Although they never got around to making a backside for the bills, nor
did they ever try to circulate them, they did give them out as door prizes at
one of their parties. They gave me one green one and three photocopied bills.
I wouldn't try to spend these if I were you. First, because you would look like
an idiot for trying to spend a photocopied twenty-five-dollar bill, and second,
because the statutes for trying to pass fake money will put you away for ten
years to life.

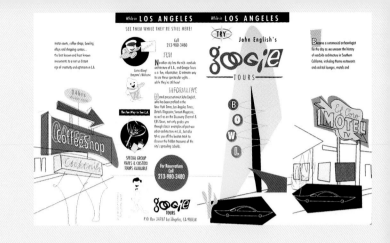

Update: John and Ginny bought a few items from my project, including my hand printed money and my *Better Homes and Gardens, Decorating Book.* In their first message to me they invited me to L.A. to take a tour of postwar commercial architecture. John runs a service called "Googie Tours", which meanders around the disappearing coffee shops, bowling allies, and tiki lounges of postwar Los Angeles. I imagined them to be retirees in their late sixties who owned a polka-dotted Partridge Family-style tour bus. In actuality they were about my age and worked with the L.A. Conservancy and as a decorator, respectively. I arrived in L.A. last fall a day early and didn't really have a plan for where I was going to stay. I called them at the last moment and they graciously let me stay on their couch for the night. That weekend we went on John's promised tour, and it was amazing to hear how much he knew about every single building that we visited. My favorite stop was the original Bob's Big Boy in Burbank, a landmark that John helped save in the nineties when a developer wanted to tear it down. The following day we ate lunch at the Silver Lake landmark Millie's, and Ginny tried to pass my twenty-five-dollar bill to the unsuspecting waitress, to no avail.

Tag # 000558
Final price: $10.49
Auction ended: May-02-01
Total bids: 7
Los Angeles, California

Tag # 000184
Final price: $16.49
Auction ended: Apr-04-01
Total bids: 13
Fresno, California

Collection of Candy: Bekah and I have been trading candy for the last eight years. We are always in search of the weirdest-looking or -tasting candies to send to each other. I don't think I have ever received the same candy twice from her. This collection features Gummy Worms in Oreo cookie dirt, a bubble-gum hot dog, root-beer-flavored Chapstick, and even some cherry-flavored Mallow Puffs. Bekah and I haven't agreed on the protocol for our candy collection; I tend to eat from my pile when I'm hungry. My personal favorite is the Gummy Roach Motel, which is a container that looks like a pesticide can filled with gummy cockroaches.

Update: Suzi never said whether or not she tried any of this candy. I recommended that she not, but I probably would if she sent them to me, so who knows?

Steel Lunch Box: No, this is not a collector's item; it's just a steel lunch box, but it does a good job holding a day's worth of food. In fact, the highest bidder on this item will receive a free lunch. Priority mail takes two to three days, and I'm willing to bet that the PB&J sandwich that I make for you will still be edible after a day or two in the mail. And the Little Debbie snack cakes will be good for a few years after you receive this care package.

Update: This was the one of the first items that Suzi bought from me; she soon became one of the folks who would bid on just about everything that I listed. She sent me pictures of her eating the lunch that I enclosed in the lunch box, PB&J as promised and an assortment of goodies from the local co-op market. Suzi made me realize the amount of trust that she had in me—I wonder if I could still send someone a lunch through the mail after all the subsequent mail-related threats? Suzi was out of the country when I drove through California. I am planning a special trip to Fresno to meet her.

Tag # 000399
Final price: $20.50
Auction ended: Jun-08-01
Total bids: 9
Fresno, California

Tag # 000956
Final price: $22.50
Auction ended: May-02-01
Total bids: 18
Los Angeles, California

Handmade Book: I made this book for my dad when I was in college. It's a collection of ads from 1940s *Life* magazines. I'm not sure what he thought of it when I gave it to him, but a few years later when I visited him in his office, he handed the book to me and told me that I must have left it in there by accident. I was so hurt/mad that I took the book back and actually covered up the inscription that I wrote in the back. I have carried it around with me since then, and am no longer mad about it. Now I give him golf balls instead. He never mistakes those for anything but a gift. Well, I thought I might give it back to him again, but maybe I will leave that up to the high bidder.

Update: I received so many letters about this book. I can tell you that I am not alone in having my handmade gifts returned at a later date from the depths of a father's office desk. Erich bought this book for his daughter Beatrix. I missed them when I made it through Los Angeles, but his friend Rachel sent me a photograph of both of them with my book. Rachel owns my dish scrubby (page 148).

Floyd's Masonry Bowling Shirt: Utica, New York, is a town where everybody bowls. Everybody! I don't think that in the entire four years I lived in the Utica area I ever met someone who didn't bowl. And I'm not talking about recreational bowling either; Utica folks are "organized" bowlers, leagues and clubs and private lanes. That may explain why, when most thrift stores in the United States have been picked clean of all of their bowling apparel, the Utica Salvation Army was chock-full of shirts previously owned by all kinds of organized Utica bowlers like Tom, Rich, Lewis, Gus, and a man named Malone, who gave up. My grandmother's maiden name was Malone; could this have been her cousin? Grandma? She never bowled, but someone in her family might have.

Tag # 000292
Final price: $22.50
Auction ended: Apr-27-01
Total bids: 8
Los Angeles, California

Update: This shirt was tight on me when I wore it, and I seldom included size information with the items that I listed on eBay. The first update that I received from Michael was one of disappointment about how small it was. A week later, though, he e-mailed me to inform me that the shirt was now owned by "a lovely young woman who was too shy to have her photo taken." His band, Gabriel Mann, offered my bowling shirt to the crowd that weekend and explained the parameters of my project. I still haven't heard from the mysterious woman, but I did keep my eye out for my shirt when I visited Los Angeles last fall.

Tag # 000253
Final price: $10.50
Auction ended: Apr-19-01
Total bids: 10
Clark, New Jersey

Canisters from My Kitchen: When I moved here I didn't really have much in the way of kitchen stuff. I found these at Kmart. They had matching spoons but someone at my inventory party tagged all of my spoons, so if you want them both you will have to buy my spoons too. I have flour in the tall one, sugar in the next smaller, cornmeal, of all things, in the next, and coffee in the smallest one. I thought that I would make corn bread all the time in Iowa, land of corn. Truth be told, I haven't opened the cornmeal container since I filled it. And now that I sold my cast-iron skillet, I don't have anything in which to make corn bread properly. Will you make me some corn bread when I visit my canisters?

Update: Rose informed me that my kitchen canisters arrived in hundreds of pieces, mixed with the flour, sugar, and cornmeal that they contained. I thought by that point that I had learned how to properly package things. I tried to refund her money but she refused to take it. She told me that she would use the broken materials to make something. I imagine a giant minimalist mosaic glued together with a flour-based paste and covered with a thin layer of cornmeal. I haven't visited her yet.

Tag # 000131
Final price: $1.25
Auction ended: May-02-01
Total bids: 2
Potomac, Maryland

Update: Ethan sent me a note from Israel; he had left my aftershave with his parents in Maryland and said that they would gladly host me if I decided to visit. I never made it to that part of the country, but I have tried to imagine what the conversation with his parents would have been like had I arrived to spend the night.

Old Spice: The closest thing that I wear to cologne is the aftershave that I get every year in my Christmas stocking. Every year it is some different brand but never more than five dollars a bottle. Brut, Old Spice, Mennen. I seldom use aftershave, so usually I make it through the entire year without finishing the bottle. This year I have discovered that many people are familiar with the scent of Old Spice. I have had a number of my women friends come up to me and ask if I was wearing Old Spice because their dads used to wear it. Now that's a bit Freudian for me, but maybe my Old Spice will work for you. I think there is still about half a bottle left.

Tag # 000230
Final price: $12.50
Auction ended: May-12-01
Total bids: 16
Los Angeles, California

Update: One day I came across a Web site called all-consuming.com, which was a detailed journal of everything that Stephanie, who bought this item, consumed in the year 2001. It was amazing—she photographed and chronicled every single thing that she purchased in a full year. There is a section where you can compute the totals that she spent on coffee, books, water, and even carrots. If you go to the archive section of the site and look through the things that she consumed on May 15, you will find a picture of her with my *Planet of the Apes* record.

Planet of the Apes Record: When people ask me whether or not I miss the stuff I have sold, they seem to be a bit skeptical when I tell them how much I miss every single thing. They say, "Come on, do you really miss your *Planet of the Apes* record or your box of Girl Scout cookies?" Well maybe not the latter, but I will miss this record. This is thrift-store gold. I paid twenty-five cents for this and it is far more valuable than that. Not just because it is collectable. It's also a reminder of midwinter Saturday afternoon broadcasting before TV sports were a twenty-four-hour endeavor, and reruns of the *Planet of the Apes* movies would play instead of professional bass fishing. Now you seldom see *Planet of the Apes* on Saturday afternoon broadcast programming. It might be because Ted Turner owns the rights to it and forgot to develop the All-Ape Network, or maybe I just have to get the super-plus digital cable satellite package to see a rerun of an old Saturday afternoon seventies classic. I will miss this record. It saw a lot of play on my radio show on WHCL in Clinton, New York.

Tag # 000189
Final price: $1.00
Auction ended: May-21-01
Total bids: 1
Los Angeles, California

Parachuting Party Favors: When I was a kid we used to sit around in the lower yard and light those green army men on fire. They would make a subtle hissing noise as they burned and a thick black smoke would fill our nostrils. As the green men burned, the plastic would melt and fall to the ground. And when the burning plastic fell it would make a zipping noise: Zip…. Zip…. Zip…. Zip…. Zip.

I think it was the noise of the fire extinguishing itself as the molten plastic fell to the dirt. It was the noise that made us do it. It was almost hypnotic. One summer we went through hundreds of green army men and even some of the gray ones that were hard to find. I guess my brothers and I would have tried to light the parachutes on fire if we had had these figures back then. I now know that that black smoke that I inhaled then is far worse for you than cigarettes, but I'm sure I wasn't alone in my enjoyment of that slow and steady flaming noise.

Update: When I was in Philadelphia, Melissa took me to a gallery opening where the artist had a bowl full of plastic cowboys and indians. I grabbed a handful of them and later mounted them on the dashboard of my car. They are made of the same soft plastic as the army men that I used to burn. For some reason we never burned our western plastic toys. I never heard from the new owner of these.

Temporama Dish Scrubby: Last February, Margaret Stratton had an artist's residency in California, and her partner didn't want her to drive out there alone. So she bought me a plane ticket from San Francisco back to Iowa, and I helped Margaret drive across the country. It was one of the best road trips I have ever been on. We stopped and visited the Edlunds, my "family" in Utah. It is so great when close friends from one place meet close friends from another. Margaret got along well with the Edlunds and they loved her too. Now Margaret knows exactly who I'm talking about when I talk about Kaya Star, Kris, Laura, Dave, Mark, Ethan, Zack, and Lisa. This scrubby contains photographs from the trip that I took with Margaret.

Tag # 000213
Final price: $32.77
Auction ended: Jun-08-01
Total bids: 10
Los Angeles, California

Update: I arrived in Los Angeles a day early and frantically called all the people who had invited me to visit, saying I needed a place to say. Rachel was the first person to answer the phone, but she was going on a date that evening, so staying with her would have been impossible. Did I really think that I could drive into the largest city in the country at seven P.M. and find a place to stay that night? I did, and I met Rachel the following day. She is a professional photographer and had recently had my Temporama dish scrubby framed. I guess she won't be using it to do her dishes with.

Tag # 000933
Final price: $1.00
Auction ended: Jun-16-01
Total bids: 1
New York, New York

Crystal Sugar, Approximately Four Pounds: Sugar, almost four pounds of sugar. I guess I won't make cookies after I sell this. I bought it more than a year ago and there is still almost four pounds of it. I guess I don't use sugar that much. I have a really tiny oven, so I can't really make cookies, and I don't take sugar in my coffee, so I never used it for that. I'm not sure how I made it so far without using even a pound of sugar. I bought this brand because of the label. If you want to market a product to me, keep the label simple and round and I promise I will buy it.

Update: I met Lindsey for a drink at the Subway Inn, in Midtown, which has now become my favorite bar in all of New York. She didn't bring the bag of sugar with her, but she did promise to make me a batch of chocolate chip cookies. She was the third person that I had met through this project and it felt a little odd meeting her for a drink in a bar. Would the rest of my journey be a series of semi-uncomfortable blind dates, one after another, all the way across the country? This one went fine; we talked about ourselves as strangers do, and after the second drink we even talked about things of substance. She knew considerably more about me than I knew about her. At some point in my stories she would tell me that she'd read about that last week on my Web site, and change the subject. As I drove across the country this continued to happen. I would show up and talk about where I had just come from and the person I was visiting would say, "Yeah, I know, I read it in your travelogue." I am still waiting for Lindsey's cookies.

Tag # 000351
Final price: $13.50
Auction ended: Apr-27-01
Total bids: 15
Ridgefield, Washington

Fly-Fishing Patch: When I was a kid my family used to spend a week each summer on the St. Lawrence River. Each year my father would try to entertain his four rambunctious boys by attempting to get them all to sit still long enough to fish. I never really liked to fish; it seemed a little pointless to me as a ten-year-old to stand still at the end of a dock and slowly reel in the line over and over and over again. I guess now I'd think it was meditative. My dad used to have his own "Bait of Champions". I'm not sure they will ever sell it in any championship bait shop, but you might be able to get it at your local market in the canned-vegetable section. He used canned corn, and it used to lure the smallest of mini-perch, bony rock bass, and if we were lucky a trout or two.

Update: I sent this to the same guy who bought my Spa City Rockers shirt (page 174). He said that even though he was disappointed with the shirt, he might hold on to the patch for a while before he throws it out.

Tag # 000693
Final price: $1.00
Auction ended: Jun-08-01
Total bids: 1
Fresno, California

Burts Beeswax Lip Balm: In February of 1999 I had more than twenty keys on my key chain, so many keys that my front pocket bulged with the awkwardly shaped institutional "do not duplicate" keys. Every time I would take my keys out I would inadvertently pull out my change and assorted pocket contents. This balm would hit the tile floor and roll down the hallway. I had to stop carrying anything in my pockets except for my keys. By that summer I had only one key left on the ring. And in July, I accidentally locked that solitary key in my car somewhere at the base of Mount Hood in Oregon. Having only one key is a great feeling. It lasted until I arrived in Iowa. On my third day here the photography department issued me eight keys, and sixteen or so keys later, and I now have more keys than I did in 1999.

Update: When Suzi won the auction on this item it was on display at the Pittsburgh center for the arts so I sent her a new container of Burt's beeswax in its place. I think that she much preferred the latter as it had never been used. When the original was returned to me I sent it to her with the next load of stuff that she bought from me.

Tag # 000557
Final price: $1.00
Auction ended: Jun-16-01
Total bids: 1
Henderson, TX

Four Syracuse China Mugs: Syracuse China is famous worldwide. It's pretty tough. If you flip over your dish in an old diner there's a pretty good chance that it was made in Syracuse. Now I guess you are more likely to see a MADE IN CHINA label, but the good stuff comes from Syracuse. When I lived there they used to have tent sales in front of the factory. Most of the stuff was overstock and the like, much of which had labels on the side from one out-of-business diner or another. These don't have labels on them, but I once saw a set of them in one of the local diners in Syracuse. I think Bekah has a set of four of these too.

Update: Angela transported the mugs from East Texas to Murfreesboro, Tennessee. As of her last message to me, the mugs were still in boxes. She said that if I made it to Tennessee she would brew some coffee for me.

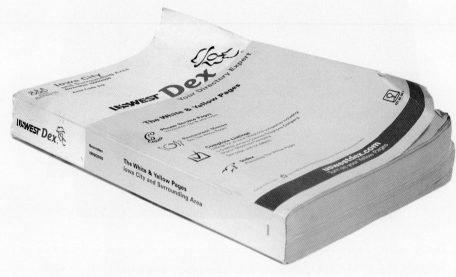

Tag # 000103
Final price: $1.25
Auction ended: Jun-08-01
Total bids: 2
Iowa City, Iowa

Iowa City Phone Book, 1999/2000: I use phone books in the type kitchen to clean ink off palette knives. I use this one to look up the number for the Motley Cow Café when I want to make a to-go order. Although I worked there for more than a year, I never memorized the number. I guess when this is gone I had better try to remember. My friend Mark's mother is a librarian. She doesn't believe in memorization. She thinks it is better to know where to find something. Why memorize the Iowa City phone book when you can own one?

Update: The high bidder on this item never paid me for it. I guess that's to be expected. I too have found myself bidding on things I don't really need on eBay. I can only imagine the high bidder receiving my $1.25 invoice for a phone book from a city they don't even live in. I ended up giving the phone book to someone in the art office at the University of Iowa. Somehow I don't think it will be accessioned into their private collection.

Tag # 000065
Final price: $18.50
Auction ended: Jun-18-01
Total bids: 10
Charleston, South Carolina

Disco Mixer: I used to own two turntables and would sit around my house in Syracuse and make tapes to trade with Bekah and Dave Broda. I don't seem to have the time to do that now. Nor do I still have two turntables. Mixing music is kind of hard. When you are making a tape you have to devote forty-five minutes to each side and have the music planned out in advance. If you make a mistake you ruin the tape. It's not like making a mix CD. I kind of miss tape making. This is a two-channel mixer with two inputs per channel, enough for two CD inputs and two turntables. I had one CD input connected to my computer and the other to my CD, and I only have one turntable now.

Update: Mike made me a mix tape and sent it to me while I was on the road. My itinerary changed so much that I think the tape was remailed from Atlanta to Iowa City and then to Salt Lake City. I sold my tape player in August, so it took me a while to even listen to it, but I can say that my mixer went to someone with a good collection of music. I never made it to the Southeast last year but plan on visiting Charleston next summer.

Tag # 000617
Final price: $34.33
Auction ended: Jun-16-01
Total bids: 12
Denver, Colorado

Wallet Book: I made this as part of an installation called *Pants*. I had five or six pairs of pants draped over the same number of chairs and created wallets for each. The wallets were supposed to be representative of the disparate groups of people that I was close to at the time and how they overlapped and fit into my life. So there was a wallet that had pictures of my mother and my brothers and sisters, a wallet that had my father and stepmother and stepsisters, and various wallets of people that I was friends with. This is the last wallet from that installation that I have left. It includes a photograph that I took of my closest friends at the time, including Trey on the lower right .

Update: I met Kendra and her brother for lunch at the Blue Bonnet in Denver, Colorado. We talked about my wallet book and I told her stories about all the people whose photographs were in the book. It was a little odd telling a stranger about where all my friends are now, and who's not friends with whom anymore. Kendra arrived with one of her favorite shirts and asked me to take it. I did and it has become one of the shirts that are always on top of the clean laundry pile.

Tag # 000160
Final price: $0.00
Auction ended: Jun-16-01
Total bids: 0

Antiseptic Mouthwash: My dad used to keep an odd-looking bottle wrapped in a manila tube under the sink in the bathroom. It was a pungent yellow liquid that was bitter to the taste and burned the inside of my mouth. Although this may burn your mouth after a while, it is far from the Listerine that my father used to use. It is green and syrupy sweet, filled with green dyes and saccharine. I think there is half a bottle now, since I took this photograph a month or so ago.

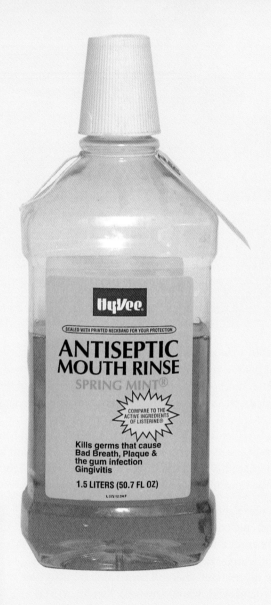

Update: No matter how many times I listed this item, no one was willing to buy it. It went to the landfill when I moved out of my apartment.

CONTACT SHEET 84

Tag # 000591
Final price: $17.50
Auction ended: Jun-25-01
Total bids: 12
Fresno, California

Update: Suzi says that this is one of her favorites now too.

Sylvia de Swaan, Contact Sheet 84: This is one of my favorite photographs. It is in a catalog of work by a central New York photographer named Sylvia de Swaan. The catalog contains images that she took upon her first return to Romania since 1945. The images often include her hand and objects of memory; they are as much about her as they are about where she is visiting. I always loved the cover photograph because it depicts such a childlike activity, pretending to fly a toy airplane, while simultaneously reminding us of the devastation of the war-torn Europe of 1945. Sylvia teaches photography at Hamilton College and I had met her a few times before I started working at Light Work. She was at nearly every opening that we ever hosted.

Jesus Night-light: Does anyone really know what the Underwriters Laboratories are? Every thing that has a plug has a UL tag on it, including this little Jesus night-light. I can only imagine what the UL headquarters must look like, a giant room with five million electrical outlets on the walls and a few hundred kids running around unplugging stuff while it's turned on. I don't think I've ever seen a product that wasn't approved by UL—except maybe this. This little false idol must have slipped through the bureaucracy. It is a bit misleading to show the night-light right side up. You see, it has a polarized plug, meaning that one prong is larger than the other, which is apparently much safer according to the Underwriters Laboratories, but in this case it means that the little lighted Lord plugs in upside down.

Update: Julie wrote me a week or two after she received her personal light-up Jesus with a complaint that Jesus only stood upside down in 40 percent of the outlets in her house. A "minority position," she stated. When I offered to refund her money she said it would not be necessary, as she had acquired the item to include in her online museum, Julie's Tacky Treasures (tackytreasures.com). Additionally, she found that the light would lie sideways in some of her outlets.

Tag # 000128
Final price: $8.00
Auction ended: May-24-01
Total bids: 9
Silver Spring, Maryland

Kembrew's Soul, New and Improved: Kembrew has been selling his soul since he was in high school. He sold one single jar of his new and improved soul for more than a thousand dollars on eBay a while back. I bought this edition of his soul for $4.95. What are you willing to pay? Kembrew sees his soul as a renewable resource, kind of like Poland Spring water. He says that he does it for the money just like everybody else.

Tag # 000544
Final price: $15.50
Auction ended: Apr-08-01
Total bids: 11
Iowa City, Iowa

Update: Kembrew's soul sold to a local artist named Jacob Hawley, the founder of the "Free Art Movement." He hosts exhibitions where everything in the gallery space can be taken away for free, and anybody can bring in new items for the taking. I found a box of some of my unsold stuff in the basement last week and left it in the gallery in a pile. Jacob also bought my Polaroid photographs (page 89), and he appropriately sent me a Polaroid photograph of the Polaroids on his wall.

159

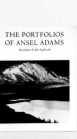

Tag # 000773
Final price: $14.50
Auction ended: Jun-16-01
Total bids: 12
Washington, District of Columbia

Update: Big Tiny was shipped to New York and then carried to D.C. Melanie sent me an update photograph of it hanging on her wall. She didn't say whether or not she ever listened to the album, but I imagine that she hasn't, as most people no longer own turntables. Will people frame old CD cases twenty-five years from now?

Big Tiny Little Record: Bob Flynt was a resident at Light Work when I used to work there. It was pretty amazing how close I became to many of the artists who participated in the artist-in-residence program. Although they were each only there for a month, I made a number of really good friends. Bob gave me this as a gift at the end of his residency. I will have to say that the music on the record is not that great but it looked really nice in this frame and has been on the wall of most of the places I have lived. I wouldn't mind getting some of the numbers out of Big Tiny Little's little black book.

ROADFOOD

The all-new, updated and expanded edition of the classic guide to America's best diners, small-town cafes, BBQ joints, and other very special eateries serving great, inexpensive regional food

JANE & MICHAEL STERN

Authors of *Square Meals* and *American Gourmet*

Roadfood **Guidebook:** Although Jane and Michael Stern have directed me to a number of pretty good restaurants, I will never forgive them for advising Trey and me to eat at the Varsity Restaurant in Athens, Georgia. Athens is a college town and has ten to fifteen great restaurants, many of which are vegetarian, and for Trey, who hadn't had one vegetarian meal since our southern tour began, the Varsity was another grilled cheese sandwich. And I highly doubt that if we lived in Athens we would ever go to the Varsity Restaurant again. Maybe Jane and Michael need to revisit Athens and offer another idea for a place to eat. Or maybe I should stop driving across the country with vegetarians.

Tag # 000704
Final price: $5.00
Auction ended: Jun-18-01
Total bids: 3
St. Paul, Minnesota

Update: Tad passes this book around the Target headquarters in Minnesota. He told me that it has become the sales representatives' bible. Whenever anyone in his office has to go on the road, Tad sends them on their way with photocopied pages from this book. I'm not sure how far the Target sales team travels, but I hope he never sends them to Athens, Georgia.

Tag # 000173
Final price: $41.00
Auction ended: Jun-25-01
Total bids: 9
Fresno, California

Update: Suzi won the sign and says it worked when she plugged it in. On August 1st I did end up going to the dump with boxes of stuff that no one would take from my curb. I ended up giving boxes of stuff to friends and put some boxes in the basement of the art building. When I left for my trip, I owned a few pairs of underwear, a pair of paints that zippered into shorts, some T-shirts, a sweatshirt, a white Honda Civic with one-hundred-thousand miles on it, and a used laptop computer. I had managed to save a few thousand dollars from the sale of my stuff, and ended up spending a third of it at the auto-repair shop before I even left Iowa.

Pulmonary Diagnostic Unit Sign: The first question that most people ask me about this project is "Are you actually selling everything?" Their second question is often "Are you replacing the stuff that you are selling?" Naturally my answer to the first question is always yes. That is the goal of the project, but I can tell you now that on August 1, when my lease is up, there will still be stuff in my house that will need to be hauled to the curb, right back to where much of what I own came from. And as for the second question, immediately after my inventory party I thought that I could get by with just selling the things that were tagged, so I continued to live my life as usual, thrift shopping and going to Surplus weekly. But I quickly realized that the only way to truly finish the project was to try to sell everything off and that I would never be able to do that if I kept accumulating stuff. This is the last thing that I bought at Surplus. I couldn't help myself, really. I knew that I could rewire it to work and so I did. I still go thrift shopping once in a while, but now I just walk around collecting all the cool stuff that I find into a pile, and then I try and convince my friends that they should buy all the cool stuff that I've found. At least someone I know would own it.

UNTAGGED
Final price: $32.50
Auction ended: Aug-04-01
Total bids: 23
San Antonio, Texas

Update: Dawn Houser is a bit of an eBay legend. It seemed like everywhere I went this fall I would run into someone who knew her or had bought something from her on eBay. In the same week in both Maine and New York City the people that I visited randomly referred to their friend Dawn Houser. I hoped to tell her about them when I made it to San Antonio, but my trip ran out of steam in Austin, less than forty minutes away.

Blue Guayabera: At my inventory party in October, I instructed the attendees to tag items that they thought were representative of my life in Iowa City. So they went through and tagged as many items as they could. At the end of the night I noticed that my favorite shirt was untagged. How is it that almost everything in my apartment was tagged, right down to my toilet paper, but the one thing that I would have tagged first remained untagged? At first I was pretty happy, because at the time I figured if it didn't get tagged I wouldn't have to sell it. But then I decided it wouldn't be true to the spirit of the project to keep things on a technicality.

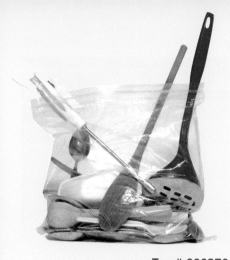

Update: When I finally went to ship Laurie her spoons, I actually decided to count them. Thirty-seven was just an arbitrary number that I came up with when I wrote the description last spring. There are really only twenty-seven spoons in that bag. Laurie lived in the Keehn Co-op at Hamilton College. I was the president of the co-op when I lived there, and it's sad to admit that some of the spoons in this bag actually came from the kitchen of the co-op in the first place. I stopped by last fall to see how they were holding up. Laurie and I didn't look for all twenty-seven of them, but my big orange ladle was in the same drawer as the little wooden spoons from my now broken and mosaiced white kitchen canisters (page 144).

Tag # 000370
Final price: $6.50
Auction ended: Jul-28-01
Total bids: 7
Clinton, New York

Bag of Thirty-seven Spoons: I had no idea what would happen when I opened my home to the fifty-odd people at my inventory party. Since some of the guests were strangers, they had to work pretty hard to come up with what items best represented me. Spoons? Well, they have been pretty hard to live without. I raided the bag last week to have a bowl of cereal, but I promise to put it back before I ship it to your house.

Saori Hoshi's Television: Saori Hoshi just completed her M.F.A. at the Chicago Art Institute. I think that she plans on returning to Japan to teach. I went to college with her and she gave me this TV/VCR when she left for Japan the first time. She used to use this TV/VCR to edit her low-fidelity videos. When I talked to her last she laughed when I told her that I still had her TV with me. One of my favorite of her videos is called *My Perpetual Existence*, in which she used traditional Japanese ink and brush to write the video's title onto the white shower tiles of her bathroom. When she went to clean the writing off, the ink had permanently stained the tiles. I returned to the Keehn Coop at Hamilton College this summer, and MY PERPETUAL EXISTENCE, BY SAORI HOSHI is still as legible as it was eight years ago.

Tag # 000003
Final price: $35.00
Auction ended: Jun-25-01
Total bids: 18
Moffett, Oklahoma

Update: Saori left the United States in January of 2002. Last week she sent me a card encouraging me to finally make Temporama international by visiting her in Japan. The new owner of her television asked to be removed from my e-mail list. I'm not sure if he ever really cared about its history.

Tag # 000024
Final price: $50.02
Auction ended: Jul-15-01
Total bids: 25
Omaha, Nebraska

Cowboy Hat: I bought this ugly hat at Artifacts in Iowa City. Mark, the owner, couldn't quite believe that anyone would buy this hat and asked me to promise not to tell the person who put it on consignment, so as not to encourage her to send him any more of those "godawful" hats. I wore this hat all over New York City last summer and continue to wear it just about everywhere I go. When I wear this hat I start to talk a little slower and people find it easier to believe that I'm from Iowa, even though I was born and raised in Syracuse, New York.

Update: Before I arrived in a town I would always notify all the high bidders in the area that I was on my way. Then I would make my plans based on the people who called me back. The new owner of my hat never called back from Omaha, so I half hoped that I would run into him on the street there, but I saw far fewer cowboy hats than I expected in this borderline western town and I never saw mine. I have never received any new information on the hat. Sometimes I walk back into Mark's in hopes of finding a new reason to talk a little slower.

Tag # 000047
Final price: $30.00
Auction ended: Jul-15-01
Total bids: 29
Homewood, Illinois

Update: As you can see from the auction date, these were some of the last things that I sold. I was western shirtless for more than two months. I finally broke down two hundred miles outside of Las Vegas. I bought a white shirt and faux suede jacket so that I could change out of the T-shirts I had been wearing all along the West Coast. Vegas seemed to require more than a beat-up T-shirt with a picture of my phone book on it.

Six Snap Western Shirts: Six snap-button western shirts, some with pearl-inlay buttons. Sara Langworthy arrived at my inventory party and went for the jugular. Everything that she tagged will be very difficult for me to sell, including these six western shirts. Most of these I found in thrift stores in Iowa City, but one I bought in Jackson Hole, Wyoming, when I drove through on my way to Mount Hood, Oregon, in the summer of 1999. My friend Krissi, a.k.a. KRS 1, took me thrift shopping there and gave me Harrison Ford's hat (page 5). I looked pretty slick with my new western shirt and Mr. Ford's hat.

Tag # 000030
Final price: $54.00
Auction ended: Jul-26-01
Total bids: 21
Oklahoma City, Oklahoma

My Last of Two Turntables: Well, this will be close to the last thing I sell. Turntables are hard to come by these days, because most people gave their records away to the Salvation Army in the eighties. And I bought them up at a quarter apiece for the last ten years. Sometimes I had to pay a buck or two for a record I wanted, but mostly I would buy a stack for five dollars or a crate for less than ten. One day Gary showed up to work with this slightly used belt-drive turntable. I set it up next to my wood-case German hi-fi turntable and bought a mixer at Radio Shack. I made some of the best tapes with that jerry-rigged setup.

Update: A rodeo DJ bought my last turntable. I can only imagine the music that now runs through the diamond DJ needle that I fitted it with last fall. Far from the jazz and disco that it was accustomed to transmitting. I never heard back from the new owner, but I'm still waiting for the tape that I asked him to make for me.

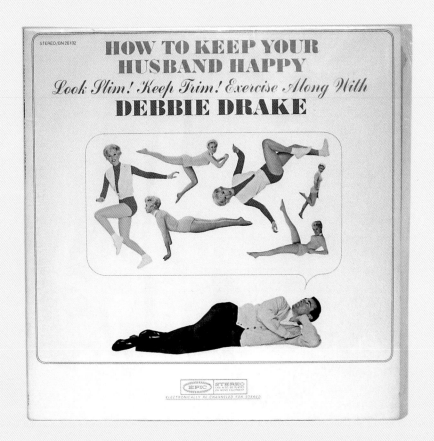

Tag # 000367
Final price: $7.00
Auction ended: Jun-23-01
Total bids: 5
Pella, Iowa

How to Keep Your Husband Happy: Now this has to be my most prized record. I'm not sure how this album was ever made, but when I found it at Johnny's Records in Syracuse, New York, I knew I had to have it. I have used samples from this album on a number of tapes, including one called *Music to Murder By*, a tape devoted to bizarre music that would either accompany or induce a desire to commit heinous crimes. Just a few short minutes of Debbie Drake could drive any emotionally stable person over the edge. Although the album doesn't include an illustrated booklet it does include a checklist for ways to keep your husband happy. My favorites are: #9, Well-set hair; #10, Mentally alert (try reading); and #2, Be at home when he arrives (if you must work, try and arrange it so you are home first).

Update: I was once quoted saying "I want to be a stay-at-home dad." Since I sent this to Catherine last summer I have been coming up with my own list of "how to keep your partner happy." Starting with: 1. Shave every day; 2. Smile at your wife (will make it more likely that she will give you your allowance); 3. Keep your newspaper neatly folded (to suggest to your wife that you actually did something today besides read the paper); 4. Stay sober until she gets home (she is more likely to listen to your stories about *General Hospital* if you don't slur your words); and, finally, 5. Take tonight's dinner out of the freezer to thaw.

Tag # 000081
Final price: $20.50
Auction Ended: Jul-23-01
Total bids: 7
London, United Kingdom

Taco Shells: Does everyone have child-hood taco memories? We never used the hard-shell type; my mom would fry up the corn shells in oil and keep them warm in tinfoil. She never seasoned the ground beef, not even with salt. Bowls of red onion, white cheddar cheese, ice-berg lettuce, and mealy tomatoes—hardly a recipe to be found in Martha Stewart. But even now when I make tacos I make them the same way. I even use canned picante sauce instead of my homemade chunky salsa. The last time I made tacos I couldn't find the soft corn shells in a can that my mom used to use, so I bought these instead because the packaging is so great. Don't be misled, there are only six shells in this partially used box.

Update: Michelle bought a few things from me and recently tried to send me photographs of where they all sit in her house. The images would only open as text files on my computer. There were hundreds of pages of characters in no particular order. Last week the hard drive where all the images from the allmylifeforsale project were stored crashed. Everything I had writ-ten, every object that I sold, and every proj-ect that I had ever worked on was backed up on that drive. For the first time in this project I realized what it would be like to really not have the things that I sold. Somehow having electronic reproductions of everything, including this box of taco shells, kept these items with me, even though the box is in Michelle's flat in London.

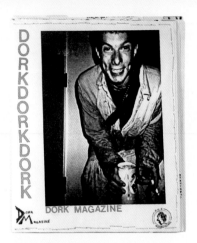

Original Master, *Dork Magazine:*
I used to make zines as often as possible when I was in college. I had a friend who worked at the library and he had access to the machine that loaded university copy cards. Every once in a while he would drop off a few cards that had 999 copies available on them. That was enough to make a small run of whatever zine we were working on at the time. We never seemed to be able to make as many copies as we wanted, so somebody always held on to the original master so we could make more copies when we were fortunate enough to get another copy card. Maybe the new owner will make the second edition of *Dork Magazine*.

Tag # 000934
Final price: $1.00
Auction ended: Jul-26-01
Total bids: 1
London, United Kingdom

Update: I think that I will always be a self-publisher; there is something about the freedom that it affords me and the creativity that is sparked by limited resources. Making a book like this one is so different from my previous experience; I'm not worried about whether or not the publisher will be able to find a few friends at Kinko's who will make some late-night copies for us. I won't have the happy accidents where a photograph slips from its taped position and creates a better composition than I intended, and hopefully my grammatical errors will be caught by the professional proofreaders.

Tag # 001010
Final price: $2.25
Auction ended: Jun-25-01
Total bids: 2
Ridgefield, Washington

Spa City Rockers T-shirt: The Spa City Rockers were the hardest hitting rock-and-roll band ever to come out of Saratoga Springs. They rocked so hard that they had to leave Saratoga and take on the hard-rock city of Portland, Oregon. Soon after, the band broke up. They were too tough, and too soon. Eric Mast gave me this T-shirt when I visited him in Portland. He threw it at me, actually, and then spat on me. Some of this is true.

Update: The high bidder on this shirt asked me to send it to a friend of his. A week after I put it in the mail I received a handwritten note from its new owner, who said that upon opening the packaging he was overwhelmed by the "musty old shirt" and decided to throw it in the trash. I really loved that shirt. But that's what happens when send your loved objects to total strangers. Eric Mast read about this tragedy somewhere on my site and sent me a new Spa City Rockers shirt when I returned from my trip. The new one is cleaner than the old one, but since it is one of my only shirts it too will become old and musty.

Old Flashbulb: I have had this for a long time. I used to keep it with my camera collection. When you collect stuff it is hard to explain why you would keep a flash that you know you will never use. Each year at the Community Darkrooms we used to have a tag sale fundraiser and every year the collectors would come out of the woodwork. The most infamous of them (to the Light Work staff) was the late John Artruba, who was also well known in the local camera stores. John Artruba had one of everything. At the tag sale he would always buy his third or fourth of whatever he bought. If it wasn't a fund-raiser I might have felt bad about taking his money when he bought his sixth broken siphon washer. He was banned from local camera stores because he would walk in on a sale and tell the customer at the counter that he had three of those and would sell one to them cheaper. The only trouble was that he would never sell anything. The customer would follow him out of the store, to his house, and by the time the price was discussed, John had changed his mind: "I couldn't sell that, then I'd only have two of 'em left." That is the guy that I could have been in fifty years. I'll sell you this flash and I don't even have another.

Tag # 001032
Final price: $3.25
Auction ended: Jul-04-01
Total bids: 2
Mountain View, Hawaii

Update: Many of the people who bought stuff from me did so with the intention of using the item that they were buying. The high bidder on this item planned on using the flash to help photograph his discovery of the world's largest lava tube tunnel ever found. I had never used the flash; in fact I had only had it on a shelf with other camera-related equipment. A week or so after I sent the package to Hawaii I received a note that voiced the new owner's disappointment with his new flash. It didn't seem to work. I hope that he eventually photographed his discovery. I'm still waiting for a photograph from Hawaii.

Tag # 001031
Final price: $16.50
Auction ended: Jun-25-01
Total bids: 15
Austin, Texas

McDonald's Polaroid Transfer: Bekah and I used to trade stuff back and forth, and one day I opened a box from NYC to find this framed picture of a McDonald's sign taken somewhere between here and Florida, not that you could tell the difference. The glass is cracked. Just like a good number of the things that, even though I have plastered with Fragile stickers, broke in the mail. When they ask me if I want insurance, I now say I do.

Update: Melanie, Rick, and Savannah have Bekah's photograph hanging on the wall in their kitchen. They were the last people that I visited on my trip across the country. I set my tent up in the front lawn of their Austin home, though they invited me to stay inside. I only camped four or five times in the ten weeks of my trip. It was much warmer outside than it would be when I returned to Iowa that week. In the morning their next-door neighbor Sam greeted me with a hot cup of coffee as I emerged from my tent. She invited me to Molly Ivins's house for a soup party with all the political left of Austin. Bekah wrote me recently to tell me that Molly Ivins is a family friend. Her photograph went to the right family.

MidAmerican Energy Bill, January 2001: So I opened my power bill this month to find that for the month of December, when I was at home visiting my family, my natural gas bill was $433.66. Who wants to buy my bill from me? Deregulation is so great, isn't it? Because when MidAmerican Energy used to have to sell at a fixed regulated rate, they sure as hell made sure their supplier made enough natural gas to go around. But when their rates were deregulated they just let the natural gas suppliers decide to lower their production of natural gas because they would just pass the cost on to me. So some natural gas supplier is now making more money than it did four years ago and I have real consumer choice: I could choose between paying MidAmerican energy $433.66 or I could have my gas shut off.

Tag # 000696
Final price: $1.00
Auction ended: Jul-27-01
Total bids: 1
Los Angeles

Update: I listed this bill three times before someone bought it. The first two times I made the minimum bid $433.66, the last time the minimum was one dollar. Brad bought the bill after he was outbid on my Latham Homes shirt. I visited him and his one-eyed dog, Jack, in Los Angeles last fall. Like me, Brad has skateboarded all of his life, and while I was there we watched a contraband copy of Stacy Peralta's skateboarding documentary *Dogtown*. Oh, and as for energy deregulation, the Federal Energy Commission is investigating Enron's role in manipulating the natural gas and electricity markets last January. Maybe I should have asked Ken Lay to pay my power bill for me.

Tag # 000381
Final price: $48.77
Auction ended: Jun-25-01
Total bids: 14
Jacksonville, Florida

Update: When Lyle received this shirt he took his daughter bowling. He reports that they bowled their highest score ever while he was wearing this shirt. It's not surprising, really; proper sporting attire can frequently enhance the way a game is played. I didn't ask him if beer was factored into his game. I'm always a little better in the second game, which I attribute to the beer consumed in the first ten frames.

U.S. Mail Bowling Shirt: Well, I think this is it, my last bowling shirt. Although it's not from Tehran, Iran, like the prize of my former collection, it is from the Jersey City U.S. Post Office Team, which really isn't that far from Iran. It has a white U.S. Post Office logo on the back and the name on the front of it is Tom. I have almost given this shirt to every Tom I know. But have decided to hold on to it for some reason. Now it's the last one I own. It is guaranteed to improve your scores on the lane or you can give it back to me when I come to visit.

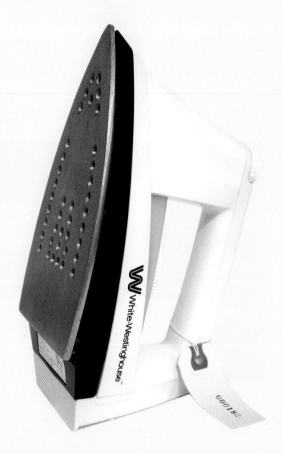

Tag # 000423
Final price: $1.00
Auction ended: Jul-15-01
Total bids: 1
Philadelphia, Pennsylvania

Update: I don't think that there is a single iron manufacturer left in the United States.

Five-Dollar Iron: When I moved to Iowa I started waiting tables at a semi-fancy restaurant. Before I realized that it would be easier to dry-clean my shirts, I thought that I needed an iron so that I could press them. So I went to a few secondhand stores and found used irons for anywhere between eight and thirteen dollars. I didn't have much money at the time so I didn't get one. The next day I was in Kmart and found this five-dollar iron. I couldn't believe how cheap it was. How could it be that a used iron would cost more than a new one? Well, if you look at where this is made you will know. Do you want my five-dollar iron?

THE PORTFOLIOS
OF ANSEL ADAMS

Introduction by John Szarkowski

Tag # 000633
Final price: $15.50
Auction ended: Jul-27-01
Total bids: 7
Brooklyn, New York

The Portfolios of Ansel Adams: I received this in high school from Jamie. I think nearly every photographer has a copy of it. In fact, most people's perception of art photography is based on the images from this book. I recommend looking a little deeper for photographers who push the envelope a little more than the grand vistas in this book. Look to places like Light Work, Camera Work, ICP, and CEPA to see what has happened in photography since the 1950s. But it can't hurt to have a copy of this book hanging around; no one will tell you that Ansel Adams couldn't take a photograph.

Update: Upon receiving my copy of this book, Ayumi dusted off her old Nikon F3 and started making images again. This fall I saw the Ansel Adams one-hundredth anniversary exhibition at the San Francisco Museum of Modern Art. Like many major exhibitions, part of the installation included a full-service exhibition store, selling everything from the catalog that Ayumi won on eBay to postcards, posters, and coffee mugs. I think museums should do away with the whole idea of exhibiting objects at all, rather they should turn their prime real estate into more profitable retail space. It would be more efficient to just exhibit and sell the exhibition-related merchandise. The new public-private partnerships could be called Walm-Art.

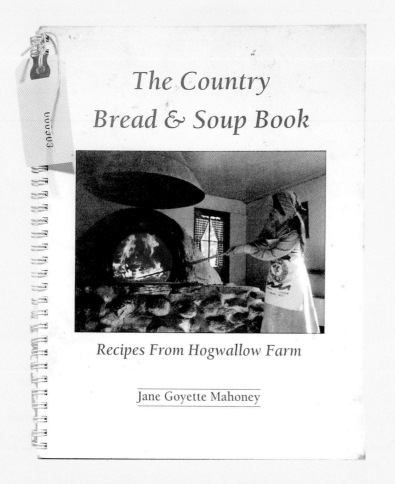

The Country
Bread & Soup Book

Recipes From Hogwallow Farm

Jane Goyette Mahoney

Tag # 000303
Final price: $12.47
Auction ended: Jul-05-01
Number of bids: 5
Salem, New Hampshire

Update: Susan bought a couple of things from me and invited me to visit last fall when I was on the East Coast. I'm not sure how our schedules didn't line up, but I never made it to Salem, New Hampshire, while she was there. I hadn't had this book for more than six months, but I have found myself making the soup recipes from memory nearly every other week. When I was randomly invited to a "soup" party in Austin, Texas, I made an adaptation of one of the recipes from this book.

The Country Bread and Soup Book: My sister's brother-in-law's family is from southern Canada, and they have run an organic farm there for years. This is a cookbook that they published a few years ago. The Hogwallow farm is nearly self-sufficient, and with soup recipes like One Flew Over the Pot and Spring Chicken Stew, your resourcefulness will meet your stomach. My favorite recipe in this book is the corn chowder, and that was before I moved to the land of twenty million ears of corn. Have you ever thought of building yourself a wood-fired oven? Well, the bread recipes here work best if you have one, but I've made some of the quick breads in my little tenement-size oven. When I make soup I seldom follow a recipe to the letter, but it's nice to have a road map.

Tag # 000257
Final price: $8.00
Auction ended: Jul-05-01
Total bids: 10
Boise, Idaho

Cool Shimmer Shirt with Hole: I found this two years ago when I arrived in Iowa. It's a great shirt except for the hole in the seam on the shoulder. I have always planned on fixing this shirt. Every time I reach for it in the closet I think that I'd better get that hole fixed. How many years will it take the new owner to sew a one-inch separation in a seam? Will they buy this, have it shipped to them, and hang it in their closet until I come and visit? Maybe we can sew it together.

Update: I visited Wendy and her husband, Shawn, last fall. She bought the shirt for Shawn even though he hadn't really worn polyester since it went out of style in the late seventies. He says that when Wendy fixes the hole in the shoulder he will start wearing it around. There was always a strange moment during my visits when people would ask me where I was planning on staying for the night. In the beginning of my trip I would sheepishly say that I didn't have any place to stay and then wait for an invitation. But by the time I arrived in Boise, I was bolder and started telling high bidders that I was planning on staying with them, either in my tent on their front lawn or on their floor. Shawn and Wendy were happy to host me. I'm not sure if the hole in the shirt has been fixed yet. We didn't sew it when I was there.

***Hawaiian Rhythm,* Luke Leilani:** I'm not sure what happened in the late fifties in Hawaii, but I do know that I have two or three identical records, with exactly the same songs on the same tracks, on the same sides. But each record is by a different band and has a different cover. I kind of think that there is only one band in Hawaii and each year they just release the same album under a new name with a different bikini-clad girl on the cover. "Hawaiian War Chant" is my favorite tune on this album.

Tag # 000354
Final price: $9.27
Auction Ended: Aug-02-01
Total bids: 5
New York, New York

Update: Mary Huhn writes music reviews for the *New York Post*. When I visited her at work last fall she gave me a tour of their offices. The best part of the tour was the framed front pages that line the walls. One of my favorites reads HEADLESS BODY IN TOPLESS BAR, and there's the more recent JENNA AND TONIC, referring to the President's daughter's run-ins with the law. Mary is a collector of just about everything. Her desk is overflowing with the hundreds of CDs that she is asked to review for the *Post*. She had just received a package from an eBay seller named Dawn Houser, from San Antonio, Texas (page 165).

Tag # 000694
Final price: $7.50
Auction ended: Jul-26-01
Total bids: 7
Fort Walton Beach, Florida

My Office Chair: I don't have an office, really, but I do have a few steel case desks, so I'm just a few cubicle walls away from working in an upstart dot-com. Well, I guess I am a bit of an upstart dot-com. I don't have any assets, have no idea what a business model is, and spend most of my time in front of a computer e-mailing my friends, many of whom happen to work (or used to work) for upstart dot-coms. This is a fine chair and it's pretty comfortable too. I will warn you, the first chair I sold cost more than forty dollars to ship, much to the high bidder's chagrin; the next chair I shipped by attaching the address label to the seat of the chair and placing $16.50 worth of stamps on the back.

Update: I boxed up the chair and a few other things that Abigail bought and sent it on its way to Florida. The shipping was in the range of fifty dollars or so. She was in high school, so I sent it to her before she paid me and told her that she could take her time paying. I think she paid me for this chair. Recently I started receiving solicitations from the Home Shopping Network telling me that my office chair would be a perfect product for their program. It further explained that items for sale on the Home Shopping Network had to have more than one thousand units available for sale. I kept trying to explain that there was only one chair and Abigail owned it, but once a week the sales rep would e-mail me again about this unique sales opportunity.

Tag # 001019
Final price: $14.27
Auction ended: Aug-09-01
Total bids: 12
Seattle, Washington

Metal Tin with Coins and Matches: At my garage sale last weekend somebody offered me two dollars for a giant glass box filled with coins. When I accepted his offer he kind of laughed, because we both knew there was more than two dollars in change in that box. This tin is also filled with coins, but it also contains the things that I could just never throw out. All the stuff that ends up in my pocket by the end of the day winds up in this tin at night.

Update: When I visited Jena in October she took the tin from her windowsill to show me what I'd left in it. When the auction ended I simply put the tin in a box and shipped it to Seattle. As we sifted through it, we found a copy of the key to the car that I was driving. Jenna took the key, opened my locked car, and started it up. One day I expect to look for my car and find a note from Jena saying that she took it for a spin. I rest easier in Iowa than I did during my few days in Seattle.

BH&G Handyman's Book: Nearly every Saturday that I lived in Syracuse, I would get up early and head out to the flea market at the Regain Market complex by old MacArthur Stadium. It was open all winter long because the buildings were used year round for agricultural distribution. My house began to fill up with stuff from that market. The highlight of each market day was the folks who ran a table in the main building. Every week at nine A.M. they would empty out boxes of stuff onto their table and about twenty of us would try and sort the gold from the garbage. By twenty after nine most of the good stuff would be bought and everything left would be sold for a dollar or two. I actually liked to buy stuff from them after the horde of people picked their choice. I think I found this book on that table after the collectors had left. I'm not sure why they didn't take this too. Usually by the end of the day the contents of this table ended up in the trash to make way for next week's overloaded boxes.

Tag # 000280
Final price: $7.50
Auction ended: Jul-05-01
Number of bids: 5
Logan, Utah

Update: Molly, who bought this and Patsy Cline's *Showcase,* is a hydraulic engineer in Salt Lake City, Utah. When I drove through last fall, I called her and asked her if she wanted to try and see Robert Smithson's *Spiral Jetty,* in the northern section of the Great Salt Lake. By the time I met up with her she had found detailed directions to where the jetty was supposed to be, and offered to guide a group of my friends and me through the desert back roads. After crossing two or three sets of No Trespassing signs, we ended up finding the site of where the jetty was supposed to be, but as Molly had predicted, it was no longer visible. So we foolishly decided to go swimming. Is it impossible to really swim in the Great Salt Lake because the water is so saturated with salt that even in a foot and a half of water we floated without touching the salt-encrusted lake bottom. We were hours away from any clean water and were covered in a thin film of crusty white salt. I felt like a freshly cooked salt potato at the New York State Fair.

Tag # 000415
Final price: $16.19
Auction ended: Jul-05-01
Number of bids: 9
Logan, Utah

Patsy Cline, *Showcase:* I'm not sure what happened to me, but at one point during my Friday evening disco show at WHCL, I started spinning Patsy Cline. My final semester as a DJ at WHCL was marked by quite a bizarre collection of music. I guess I had exhausted the supply of disco and funk at the Utica Salvation Army. I started to buy thumbed-over records from other genres and mix them in with the rest of my music on the show. She is pretty great and this has them all—"I Fall to Pieces," "Crazy," and "Fooling Around."

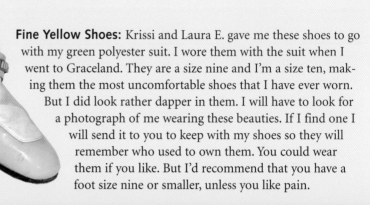

Fine Yellow Shoes: Krissi and Laura E. gave me these shoes to go with my green polyester suit. I wore them with the suit when I went to Graceland. They are a size nine and I'm a size ten, making them the most uncomfortable shoes that I have ever worn. But I did look rather dapper in them. I will have to look for a photograph of me wearing these beauties. If I find one I will send it to you to keep with my shoes so they will remember who used to own them. You could wear them if you like. But I'd recommend that you have a foot size nine or smaller, unless you like pain.

Tag # 000327
Final price: $21.92
Auction ended: Jun-25-01
Total bids: 18
Chicago, Illinois

Update: When I arrived in Chicago I thought that it would be fun to try to meet all of the high bidders in Chicago in one place. So I invited all of them to join me for the taping of a local public-access television program. *Chic-A-Go-Go* is a children's dance program for kids of all ages, a cross between *American Bandstand*, *Sesame Street*, and the good Lollapalooza. I'm not sure what I was expecting, but only two of the twenty or so high bidders attended the taping, and the owner of these shoes wasn't one of them. They would have looked nice with the pink shirt that I wore that day.

Tag # 000589
Final price: $20.50
Auction Ended: Aug-07-01
Total bids: 17
Chicago, Illinois

Franny and Zooey, J. D. Salinger: I never read *The Catcher in the Rye*. There is so much that I should have read but haven't. How did I graduate from high school, much less college?

Update: Dawn and Ted were the only two people from Chicago area that joined me at the taping of *Chic-A-Go-Go*. The following day they invited me to their house for dinner. We talked about how they met over the Internet and decided to move to Chicago together from other parts of the country. I was curious to find out what it was like to meet somebody over the Internet, but then realized that I was staying in the houses of total strangers I had met the same way. Dawn and Ted corresponded for over a year before they met in person. And here I was in their house eating dinner two weeks after they bought my copy of *Franny and Zooey*. Dawn gave me her copy of *The Catcher in the Rye*.

Update: Michelle bought my camera, the photos, and my original master of *Dork* magazine. I sent her the camera loaded with unprocessed film. When she finally had the film processed at the lab she said they sent her home with the wrong person's photographs. How would she know? Well, I guess my roll of film was unlikely to have pictures of Brits at birthday parties. I don't know what was on that film. I hope it didn't have pictures of my visit to Niagara Falls with Sasha and the heart-shaped tub....

The T-4 Super and Fifty Photographs: This is the best camera that I have ever owned. I have convinced at least ten of my friends to buy a T-4 Super for themselves. I know professional photographers who occasionally even do work for hire with the T-4 Super. I have taken thousands of photographs with this camera. It is small enough to fit in a pocket and has a Carl Ziess lens. When my friend Paul, who is a photographer in New York City, found out that the T-4 was going to be discontinued he went out and bought two just in case the two that he has ever break. I carry this camera around with me everywhere I go. I have taken pictures with it in nearly every state in the country, as well as in Sweden, Norway, and Canada. This item includes fifty photographs taken with the T-4 super.

Tag # 000094
Final price: $153.50
Auction ended: Jul-26-01
Total bids: 31
London, England

My Last Radio Show, 88.7 WHCL: This is the tape of my last radio show at 88.7 WHCL in Clinton, New York. It was a Friday afternoon show where I played mostly my records from the Salvation Army. I haven't listened to this in a while, but if practice makes perfect this should be the best radio show I ever had. College radio is the last vestige of freedom on the airwaves. But even on college campuses they are starting to subscribe to format radio services. Why the hell would a college student want to play songs picked by a corporate record executive?

Update: Throughout this project there has been a weird sense of synchronicity between the participants and myself. As I sat down to write this update, thinking I'd have to make something up, I received a message from Steve, the new owner of the tape. He reminded me that I was a little bit "in-da-house-yo" during my final show. By which I think he means to say that I was sending out "shout-outs" as if I were a DJ on Hot 97. It's a little embarrassing to remember myself as a privileged, overeducated white kid sending "shout-outs" to my friends "in-da-house" at three-thirty on a Friday afternoon.

Tag # 000250
Final price: $10.50
Auction ended: Aug-07-01
Total bids: 10
San Francisco, California

Tag # 000571
Final price: $31.00
Auction ended: Aug-07-01
Total bids: 22
Staten Island, New York

Update: Phil is a professional wrestler and now owns my Sahara ashtray. I'm not sure if he smokes, but I never did and I still owned five or six. I wonder if he ever wrestled in Las Vegas. I meant to try and meet up with him on the Staten Island Ferry when I was in New York last year. I think Chinese food and Bud tall boys on the Staten Island Ferry could be considered the perfect filter date in New York City. It's free, and if things don't work out you can be back in Manhattan in less than an hour.

Unsold Ashtray: Last weekend I took all the stuff that didn't get tagged at my inventory party and brought it all out to my front lawn for the first-ever allmylife yardsale. For two days I sat in 105-degree heat and tried to convince the good people of Iowa that they needed what was on my lawn. By the second day I was giving stuff away. And by four P.M. on Sunday I had hauled the remainder to the curb and was upstairs in my apartment in the air-conditioning. This was at my curb overnight and no one took it. I love this ashtray; it's from the Sahara in Las Vegas, which no longer exists. Surely there is somebody who wants this. Even if my fellow Iowans wouldn't take it for free.

Tag # 000579
Final price: $32.00
Auction ended: Aug-07-01
Total bids: 9
Boston, Massachusetts

Update: Karin sent me an update including a photograph of her own little phone books. She still hasn't decided what to do with mine but she told me that she has ruled out stalking the people whose numbers and addresses are still current. That was nice to hear.

Little Phone Books: These little phone books are pretty much useless to me as far as finding my friends' phone numbers. Everyone I know has moved at least twice since I filled these books. But they are a really good reminder of who I was back then. I started looking through these when I photographed them and remembered the people that I used to be friends with.

THE OFFICIAL GUIDE TO
OUTDOOR SKATING

Tips for all skaters
from beginner to expert
Step by step approach
shows you how
to get from here
to there with speed,
style and flash

Frank Simcoe

Tag # 000421
Final price: $3.25
Auction ended: Aug-02-01
Total bids: 4
San Pedro, California

Outdoor Skating **Book:** My mom sent me this book when she found out that I was an avid skateboarder. At fourteen the connection between late-seventies roller-skating and skateboarding was far from apparent. But since then I have bought a pair of disco style skates, and once in a while I don my orange eight wheels at the skate park. I like to make fun of Rollerbladers at the park by mimicking their tricks on my late seventies skates; nothing is more embarrassing than to be compared to the guy on the cover of this book. Although I do kind of wish that I could grow a mustache like that.

Update: Terry is an avid roller skater and bought my book for its instructional value. I only appreciated its ironic value; I'm glad that it has a home where it is looked at for more than a quick laugh at the past. My parents sold my roller skates at their garage sale last summer, that and everything else that I left in their house. I guess it's only fair; I did sell their Christmas gifts last year.

Tag # 000424
Final price: $5.50
Auction ended: Jul-28-01
Total bids: 2
Brooklyn, New York

Life magarine, Skateboarding Issue:
This is my most prized *Life* magazine.
Complete with a photograph of a priest
on a skateboard, while far from a papal
endorsement of the sport, it's the reli-
gious validation that a former skateboarding altar boy needs. I will only sell
this to somebody who still skateboards.
It needs to stay in the family, so to
speak. Maybe somebody from the Silly
Pink Bunnies gang will be its new
owner.

Update: Reggie works for the Brooklyn Museum of Art. This was the second item that he bought from me. It wasn't until I arrived in New York City this summer that he realized I was different from most other eBay sellers. "You want to visit your *Life* magazine?" he asked me over the phone. I explained what I was doing and he offered to give me a tour of the museum. He is responsible for public relations at the museum, and since his name appears on all of its press releases, he is the primary recipient of any mail that the museum receives. The controversial *Sensation* exhibition yielded mailbags full of handmade cards from Catholic schoolchildren who forgave Reggie for his museum's "blasphemy".

Tag # 000154
Final price: $2.25
Auction ended: Jul-15-01
Total bids: 5
Annapolis, Maryland

Update: My cousin Patrick was the high bidder on my cooler and my plan was to hand-deliver it to him when I made it to the D.C. area in mid-September, but my plans changed and I never made it to Annapolis. I am two days older than Patrick; our mothers must have been in a race to give birth that year and my mother won. Each year in our extended family one family would wrap up my grandfather's terrible green fish painting and give it to another family member, who would have to hang it in their house for the next year. I think I will send Patrick this cooler for his birthday next year.

Road Trip Cooler: I'm not sure where I even got this, but it has certainly served me well. It fits right on the hump between the backseat and the emergency brake. I usually fill it with cheese and cans of Coke. I don't have air-conditioning in my car, so it is really great to have some cold beverages when I drive long distances. I once drove from New York to Salt Lake City without really stopping. It was a thirty-seven-hour drive, and by the time I got there, I was barely awake. When I drive alone I try to drive as far as I can without stopping. I usually plan to stop only when I need to get some gas, and since my car gets about thirty to forty miles to the gallon, that's a long time between stops. It was a little difficult when I had my thermos full of coffee. But now that someone in the Bronx owns my thermos, I may not need to take as many bathroom breaks.

Tag # 000036
Final price: $18.52
Auction ended: Jul-27-01
Total bids: 13
New York, New York

Tiffany Flask from My Brother's Wedding: I received this Tiffany flask from my brother Mike when I participated in his wedding. I was on my way to Salt Lake City to pursue a career in higher education (a.k.a. snowboard instructing). I think his wedding was the last time that I have worn a tuxedo. I think there is still a drop of something in there, but I'm not sure what it is. It was late that night when I had the bartender fill it up. If he had been doing his job right he would have filled it with water.

Update: A week after Maya received this flask in the mail, her roommates passed it around and found the flavor of its contents quite disgusting. It now sits on the shelf in her room appropriately empty. On September 10, 2001, I visited Maya in her old apartment on Canal Street. Her next-door neighbor invited us over to watch an electrical storm as it blew in from the Hudson River. The next morning I woke up at seven A.M. without the alarm clock and left her house by eight for my six-hour drive to Boston.

199

Allmylifeforsale.com Domain Name: This is the final item for sale on allmylifeforsale.com. Although there are still a few boxes of things left that remain unsold, my lease is up, my apartment is empty, and this sale is over. Over the last six months my life has changed in subtle ways. I no longer own my favorite clothes, have been eating out for the last month straight, and no longer have much tying me to Iowa City. In the next few months I plan on visiting as many high bidders who invited me to visit as I can. I will not sell this domain name to a for-profit company. Ideally I would love to see the high bidder on this item use it again for the same purposes that I did. I will give you the templates that I built the site with and will help you get started if you like.

Update: The University of Iowa Museum of Art won my final auction. They took control of the site on January 1, 2002, and plan to maintain the site, as is, for a period of at least ten years. In the agreement that we worked out, they technically only own the domain name and none of the content of the site. However, I have decided to allow them to host the content for as long as they like. I had to write a letter to the Iowa Board of Regents explaining exactly what it was the museum was purchasing from me. I think that they were a little confused by the whole matter. I tried to explain that it was as if they were purchasing a painting from me, but I think it was hard for them to relate to the idea that a museum could simply purchase a name. Alaina recently registered the domain name AMLFS.com and plans to do the project again in Australia; I guess she will have to sell my Pez dispensers (page 85).

Last Item to Sell
Final price: $1,165.00
Auction ended: Aug-11-01
Number of bids: 34
Iowa City, Iowa

Subject: G.O.B.
From: Ashley@—
To: john@temporama.com

Dear John:

(Man, the thrill never wears off of writing that, though it must have stopped on reading it for you quite a while ago.)

Your Great Old Box is still fabulous and no worse for wear, and we are getting ready to set off for London, Sweden, and Majorca tomorrow morning. I was having him send postcards at first but then I thought it would be better to just collect stuff inside and a journal with words and photos from wherever we went and then whenever you get him back you can just check it all out then. So don't think we have forgotten you, or that he has settled down into a life of boredom or retirement in tiny Chester Springs. Oh no, my friend. JF's GOB has only begun.

I am sad to see your domain name sale ending on the day I will be traveling home from Sweden, as it was my dream to be like you and rid myself of all my possessions. Well, at least to be like you in the respect that I would have rid myself of all my possessions. Alas, I will be too busy to sit around trying to outbid people, and besides all that cutthroat shit is not my style. But with any luck I will come home and have a nice salad with my roommate Mike, who is bidding with great ferocity for your Vidalia onion.

Good luck with the rest of your sale and I hope you make it to Philly when you are all done. Let us know if you need any gas $$.

Ashley
Chester Springs, Pennsylvania

Subject: Latham Home Shirts
From: Katherine@—
To: john@temporama.com

John,

After resorting to some rather cutthroat bidding methods, I am now the proud owner of your Latham Homes T-shirt. I got the shirt because a) I voted for Nader (coming from a family of straight-ticket Republicans!) and b) I'm a big fan of homes! Latham or otherwise … Actually, I just really like your project and wanted to take part.

Would you consider visiting me on your trip? I'm not a murderer or looking for a new boyfriend, but I really would like to meet you and talk with you about what you're doing. I'm absolutely fascinated by the whole thing. I am in graduate school for theology, just east of Los Angeles. I'm going after a Master of Divinity degree (isn't that a weird title?) in hopes of being a hospital chaplain someday, and then later perhaps a pastor.

Jesus talked a lot about selling one's possessions and I am interested in any spiritual insight you might gain once this project is complete and you're living free of stuff. Anyway, I think we could have a very interesting time.

Thanks!
Katherine
Claremont, California

Subject: Belly Dance Lessons
From: Sean@—
To: john@temporama.com

Hey John,

I will have pictures of the *How to Belly Dance for Your Husband* album soon. I'm getting married in September and I plan to present my wife-to-be with this fine album from your life.

I'm going to give it to her at our rehearsal dinner. It's in the process of being framed at the moment and I'm trying to digitize the album as well.

Please consider yourself welcome to visit if you can make it to Hampton, Virginia. We have plenty of room and as added incentive if you do make it, the Fabio ICBINB (I Can't Believe It's Not Butter) is yours, my friend.

Keep me posted!!!

Sean
Hampton, Virginia

E-Mail Updates

Subject: Jesus Night-light
From: Julie@—
To: john@temporama.com

Dear John:

I can't say that I'm entirely satisfied with the Jesus night-light. First of all, the lightbulb that came with it doesn't work. But what's really bothering me is that the description of the item didn't match up with reality. In an array of tests performed in my house, rivaled only perhaps by the rigorous testing of Underwriters Laboratories (www.ul.com), I found that in 65 percent of the

outlets in my house, Jesus stood upright, 30 percent of the outlets required Jesus to hang upside down as promised in your description, and a mere 5 percent of my outlets caused Jesus to assume an alternative position. It is this minority position, if you will, that is represented in the photo attached to this e-mail.

But hey, while a lot of your feedback seems to credit your cast-off items with changing the correspondents' lives, I never had such high expectations for the $11.50 I spent. Caveat emptor. I did hope to display the night-light on my Web site, "Julie's Tacky Treasures," but now I'm wondering how it would fit, given the inconsistent or perhaps inconclusive results of my testing.

Maybe this is just another example of God working in mysterious ways, as the nuns used to tell me: a theological dilemma, or perhaps His way of making a joke. I've developed a personal philosophy, since becoming a recovering Catholic, that God definitely can laugh at Himself (when He's not laughing at us). I believe He has a sense of humor, unlike the guys I've met through the personal ads who SAY they want a woman with a sense of humor when what they mean is that they want a woman who will laugh at THEIR jokes. But I digress …

In closing, John, I probably will continue to scan your Web site for potential tacky treasures, and even bid on a few when the opportunity arises.

Julie, Curator,
Julie's Tacky Treasures (tackytreasures.com)
Silver Spring, Maryland

———————

Subject: Las Vegas Glass
From: Elle@—
To: john@temporama.com

John,

I bought the Vegas glass in December, maybe? I lobbied for the Vegas glass long and hard, mostly because of John Freyer's story.

Last July, five months after John got this glass from Micah, I made a many-hour drive to Vegas to almost get married, and instead we broke up a month later and I moved back east. I don't know why I bought the glass; I felt a weird connection to it.

Either that or I was simply attracted to the gold foil. I was going to send this glass to my ex, but when I got it in the mail from Mr. Freyer, it was broken. Thus is the risk of mailing glassware, I guess.

The glass is still in the box it came in, hidden under my bed, in about five different pieces. I was going to glue it back together, but that seemed sacrilegious. If not sacrilegious, at least a little wrong. So it's still waiting for something under my bed. I don't know what.

Elle
Washington, DC

Subject: Your Ring.
Date: Sun, 22 Jul 2001
From: Emily@—
To: john@temporama.com

Hey John,

So, the ring. The only ring you've every worn. I've watched you put all kinds of things up for sale with a knot in my stomach. I guess I never realized how much sentimental value some things hold until I started reading your descriptions of your stuff. Anyway, the ring was too much: it struck a chord with me, and I had to bid. See, I keep all of my old rings. Not that I've had many, but I've had a few important rings throughout my life (that for whatever reason I don't wear anymore), and they all stick around, even when clothes, pictures, music, etc. from that particular era wear out, get sold, or just get lost.

So anyway, I bid on your ring. And it stays in a cedar jewelry box with a bunch of my rings and other assorted things that aren't useful but can't be discarded (it's the one on the right in the picture). It's in the box because my room is always so cluttered—much like the box—that it wouldn't have a chance otherwise. Even today that very box is under a stack of records under two books under a drum machine under three shirts. So don't think it's been placed there carelessly.

So stop in Columbus along your way if you can, and wear the ring home, ultimately, I think it belongs back on your hand. Until then, it's safe here, in a box on my dresser in my room. And yeah, at your suggestion, occasionally I wear it (I'd wear it more if it weren't a little bit too big) when I need a reminder that someone somewhere is saving this world.

Emily
Columbus, Ohio

Subject: re: Japanese Design
From: Susan@—
To: john@temporama.com

Dear John,

I was over the moon to receive the Japanese design book from my dad. I collect anything and everything associated with the 1970s and also have a keen interest in graphic design, which I studied at college. I have had quite a few offers to sell the book but there is no way I will ever part with it as it has become "part of my life not for sale". It now has pride of place on my bookshelf and I love to tell the story of how I acquired it through your brill Web site.

Susan
Tyne & Wear, United Kingdom

———————

Subject: Al and Irene BBQ
From: Dave@—
To: john@temporama.com

Dear John,

The T-shirt arrived safe and sound here at work and is a firm favorite already! People keep asking me, "Where's Al and Irene's then?" Well, it's at Cedar Rapids isn't it! Not really knowing where that is, I must visit one day to really know and to see what the place actually looks like.

So if anything, apart from sporting a new bright yellow T-shirt (I wouldn't normally wear a yellow one!), the T-shirt has given me a strange but nice connection to Cedar Rapids and a desire to know more about it.

Good luck with your project. Take care and stay in touch and say a big hello to all at Al and Irene's BBQ Shack.

Dave
London, United Kingdom

Subject: Your Birthday
From: Brian@—
To: john@temporama.com

John,

Well, I won one of the more difficult things to comment on as far as how it's affected my life. Since I can't "use" the item, I'll just give you an idea of how my life has changed since December 28, 2000.

When I moved to New York I didn't know anyone. I got here, my plans for a job didn't work out, I wasn't having much luck making friends, and overall I was pretty lonely. But this was loneliness I've not experienced the equal of since the misery that is junior high school. Something about knowing no one and having no one to talk to, confide in, or share with in a city of millions, where there is always something exciting or interesting to share or experience, intensified the feeling. And if you're not careful, you start to feel more and more lonely; you get less and less motivated and slowly withdraw into a shell of self-pity. It's pretty pathetic.

In late December I was feeling like I had had enough of this and I was willing to try anything. Then I stumbled across your Web site, bid and won your birthday, and it actually changed who I am. I went to the party, met your friends, and had a great time, but it didn't end there. I also met up with some of them after it was all over and we continued to have good times. Slowly I was making friends. Your friends.

I disagree with the idea that I purchased your friends from you. Your relationship with each of them remains intact and I simply formed friendships. But in a way, I unwittingly used you as a search agent to meet them and then get to know them. I can only imagine how, at least partially, it must be/have been unsettling to have sold the experience of being you at your birthday, a quantified, almost contained length of time, and then see that stranger sort of leak outside the box. The terms of the purchase were for that night, and that night alone, but I'm somehow still here.

I don't feel that I have a conclusion to wrap this all up with. There's not a clear lesson here since it wasn't a simple transferral of property as is much of the rest of your project, but this experience has definitely changed my life. Arguably the true essence of who we are is purely the culmination of our experience, and since I did pay for the initial contact and I've now spent four months interacting with some of your close friends, then perhaps I actually did buy something of you and have incorporated it into myself.

But I don't think it's as clear cut as all that. When you sell a typewriter or a brick you are giving away something that you may consider being part of who you are. That thing no longer has a place in your life and does have a place in the life of someone else, opening up the potential for the buyer to experience something of yours and merge it into his or her own life. However, when you dabble with a true chaotic and unpredictable force, people, you cannot confine it to the role of an object. While I did have the birthday and got to experience that in a finite manner, something unexpected happened. Friendships were formed and they grew out of that initial contact. Although the purchase provided the medium, the resulting relationships were more than simply my co-opting something of yours and making it my own. They were the unpredictability of human interaction. The surprising and uncontrollable dynamic of people.

So my purchase was one of the anomalies. I got exactly what I bid on and it fulfilled the expectations I formed from your Web site, but since some aspects of my purchase were alive and able to interact with me, it opened up possibilities that can never be explored with a chair or a shirt. Not only did I get a thing, the experience at the party, I also got an opportunity. You exposed more of your world by allowing me a short time to spend with your friends than anyone who gets to keep an object of yours indefinitely.

So I feel that I should thank you. You took an incredible risk with this experiment and aside from what you may learn through the project (and the cash you make) there is little room for personal gain. I, on the other hand, paid $1.25 and met people who've become some of the best friends I've ever known. That's something that will stay with me forever.

Brian
New York, New York

_____

Subject: U.S. Army Chair
From: Milan@—
To: john@temporama.com

Mr. Freyer:

This is a belated note to thank you for your gift of the U.S. Army chair to our Franklin Furnace collection; in fact, we are so pleased to have it that it's already on display as part of a small exhibit we've done commemorating the twenty-fifth anniversary of the Archive. So add us to your map of where your life is on display—MoMA library, 6th floor … Regards and best wishes on your projects.

Milan R. Hughston
Chief of Library & Museum Archives
The Museum of Modern Art

Subject: Phone Books
From: Karin@—
To: john@temporama.com

John,

Hi, sorry my response as to what I've done with "my little phone books" and how possessing them has affected me has taken this long but I'm still trying to figure it out. Have you ever seen the movie *Ghost in the Machine*? Where this guy goes through Karen Allen's address book systematically tracking down and terrorizing everyone listed? Was it Karen Allen? Anyway, I've ruled that out as an option.

I thought maybe I'd find a familiar name inside, like the six degrees of John Freyer or something, but I didn't. Maybe I'll use the names/info therein to pad worthy petitions, or I was thinking that I should use the address books as some sort of primary source, do a study on what seemingly innocuous lists of friends and relatives can reveal about a man's life—which could lead perhaps to the first J. Freyer biography.

Really, I don't know what I'll do with them but already something good has come out of this transaction—as shown in the picture attached, we've managed to reunite two long-lost brother address books separated at their manufacture … yours left, mine right. If you need any more input or still want to stop over in Boston, let me know.

Thanks,

Karin
Boston, Massachusetts

Subject: Bowling Shirt
From: Michael@—
To: john@temporama.com

John,

Here is a photo of me finding a better home for the Floyd's Masonry bowling shirt. My band (Gabriel Mann) was playing a show at the Mint in Los Angeles.

I offered the shirt up to anyone that was willing to come up and claim it. It was claimed by a lovely young woman who was too shy to have her photo taken, so you just get me. For more info on the band, if you're interested, check out gabriel-mann.com.

Michael
Los Angeles, California

_____

Subject: Your Film and Ribbon
From: Kiem@—
To: john@temporama.com

John,

Yep, the blue ribbon will again reside in your hometown, Iowa City. They must have really wanted your ribbon. They e-mailed me a few times too and offered me enough to let me let it go.... It's been forwarded to Donna in Iowa City, Iowa.

As for the rolls of unexposed film: Two of the rolls didn't produce anything. One was too old and the other apparently wasn't exposed. The other three seem to be of you and friends on a snowboarding/ski trip.

Klem
Albany, California

Subject: Purple Sweater
From: Keith@—
To: john@temporama.com

John,

Your girlfriends' favorite sweater now watches the goings-on at my auto-supply/sign shop here in beautiful old town Newark, Texas.

As you will notice, she has a revered place among my assorted collectables. I placed a garment bag over her to protect her from conditions one might expect here. (This was in no way an attempt at a mercy killing, in spite of the obvious moth holes.)

This may seem like a dull and boring life for something that no doubt has seen a few wild times. Well…. it is.

Sorry, that's life! I mean, I'm stuck here too! Will keep you posted on any big changes that occur.

Keith
Newark, Texas

_____

Subject: Bag of Corn
From: Sandy@—

To: john@temporama.com

John,

What fun we had with the squirrel corn. The kids were really excited with the corn project. After just a little encouragement, they had a blast putting it out and watching the squirrels eat it. We decided to put it out one at a time so the squirrels wouldn't pig out.

Sandy
Lynnwood, Washington

Subject: Planet of the Apes
From: S E H @—
To: john@temporama.com

Hi John,

I admit I hadn't checked your site for a while, and I'm really bummed out for not doing so. I bought the *Planet of the Apes* record from you 5/15/01, and would have loved for you to visit us.

I have read some of your travelogue and enjoyed it very much. Your project is also so much about connecting with other people, and often mine is myopic, reflecting my personal disconnect. Opposite sides to the same coin? Or not? Dunno. Anyway, I live in Echo Park (next to Silverlake) in L.A., and often go to Millie's. I've always meant to get to that Bob's Big Boy in Burbank too.

Also of note, I was in NYC on Sept. 11. I opted to keep up with my project, because I felt my purchases on the day of & days following were sort of telling (like looking at the situation using a Fresnel lens or microscope or something). It's great you documented your experience as well, very visceral....

No leads on the all2consuming yet. I'm also considering other ways to either expand the idea or look at consumption from a different angle (food, sex, disease, obsession, or something fun like that).

Best,
Stephanie (all-consuming.com)
Los Angeles, California

Subject: Answering Machine
From: Morgan@—
To: john@temporama.com

Hey John.

Well, the truth is I haven't used your answering machine tape yet nor do I plan to use it in the near future; it's something I'm keeping for when I feel the urge to use it.

I'm a musician and producer and I've long been fascinated with the idea of using spoken word or even samples of spoken word in music, and while that's been explored in techno and some rap, not too much in the more rock/groove/jazz-oriented world.

So when I find that a tune or some tunes call for any of the stuff that was on your answering machine, I'll use it. It is cool though. You seem like a really neat guy, if based on nothing else than your Web site, this project, and the various messages people have left you on your machine.

And there's someone on your machine who left like five consecutive messages going off about the pros and cons of Ralph Nader that, well, on second thought maybe I'd better not say anything about that, but it is possible that you and I might be thinking the same thing about that.

Catch ya later,

Morgan
Commerce, California

Subject: Cheeseburger with Sara Langworthy
From: Service@ebay.com
To: john@temporama.com

Dear John D. Freyer,

EBay appreciates the fact that you chose to list your auction: 543023266 George's Burger w/Sara Langworthy, allmylifeforsale with us.

However, we do not allow auction listings to be used for any purpose other than auctioning of an item. Auction listings that do not offer an item will be ended early by eBay.

Therefore, we have ended this auction and all fees have been credited to your account.

eBay Service
San Jose, California

Subject: Ruby-Red Chair
From: Alex@—
To: john@temporama.com

John,

Well, the chair made it—yes, in one piece. I don't use eBay, my friend Cordelia was the one who bought it for me. It's in my room and is quite comfortable in my humble opinion.

I don't know how they delivered it, but for reasons unknown to me, the mailperson put it under my doormat. It was the weirdest-looking thing. They (the Post Office) also put three or four stickers on it apologizing because they thought they had torn it up during shipping. Ever since I saw your Web site I wanted something from it, and now my wish has come true. You are like Richard freakin Simmons!

Alex
Simi Valley, California

Subject: re: Pasty Cline
From: Molly@—
To: john@temporama.com

John,

I just wanted to let you know that the first night I got her, Patsy and I sat on my front porch, singing our hearts out to the mountains about cheating men and lost loves, and drank several margaritas on a hot summer evening. There ain't nothing better in life. The 1950s-era *Handyman's Book* goes perfectly with my 1950s-era cookbook by the same editors. Being a handy gal myself, I found the suggestions rather humorous—very male oriented. Reminds me of an irrigation job I did a few weeks back where the old man told me that I was going to make myself a handy house-wife someday. I can only dream. You are more than welcome to visit your things—that is, if you want to be holed up in a small town in the mountains for a while.

Oh, and if you can't stand drinking beer that's half the alcohol content of the rest of the world, I suggest you keep your distance.

Ciao,

Molly
Logan, Utah